A world of Ferns

Josephine M. Camus · A. Clive Jermy
Barry A. Thomas

NATURAL HISTORY MUSEUM PUBLICATIONS

In gratitude to the late Dr R. E. Holttum (1895–1990)
who understood ferns better than anyone else.

PRESIDENT OF THE BRITISH PTERIDOLOGICAL SOCIETY 1960–1963

Stag's horn ferns, such as this *Platycerium grande*, can be grown outside in warmer, frost-free temperate regions.

NWSt
1ADK1342

First published 1991 by
Natural History Museum Publications
Cromwell Road, London SW7 5BD

© J. M. Camus, A. C. Jermy & B. A. Thomas, 1991

Designed by Gilliam Greenwood

A catalogue record for this book is available from the British Library

ISBN 0 565 01120 0

Type set in Goudy Old Face by Tradespools Ltd, Frome, Somerset
Printed in Singapore by Craft Print Pte Ltd

Pictures on Cover, Inside Front and Inside Back Cover, see pages 64, 106, 31 respectively.

CONTENTS

The scaly male fern (*Dryopteris affinis*), a common woodland fern in western Britain and an attractive species to adorn the garden.

PREFACE

Epiphytic ferns festooning a tree in Singapore

Most people recognise a few ferns, knowing them as feathery-leaved plants growing in shady places, but few have any idea of just how amazing in form and extraordinary in life-style ferns can be. There are many excellent books which illustrate those found in particular countries or regions, but their appeal is largely to the committed fern-enthusiast or to horticulturalists. This book introduces the wealth of variation in ferns through their natural habitats to encourage the reader to take more interest in this group of fascinating plants.

The three of us have all been studying ferns and their allies for a long time and have been privileged to serve on the committee of the British Pteridological Society in a variety of ways for many years. This book commemorates a special year, the Society's first centenary.

The Society was founded in 1891 by a small group of fern enthusiasts at a meeting in the English Lake District. At first it catered for gardeners and plant collectors whose interests in ferns and their varieties had, no doubt, been fired by the 'fern craze' which had swept Victorian Britain thirty years earlier. One hundred years later the Society is still flourishing. Its membership now comprises botanists and gardeners, both amateur and professional, from all over the world. Their interests span taxonomy, classification, evolution, ecology and conservation as well as the traditional delight in growing ferns. Without the continued zeal of our members, many of the fine Victorian varieties discovered by our predecessors would have been lost to future generations of gardeners.

We are also fortunate in having an enthusiastic membership that supported us in producing this book. The beautiful photographs, taken by our members and friends, were all given free for our use so that the Society might benefit from this publication and thus promote an interest in ferns in a variety of ways throughout its centenary year. It was, of course, possible to use only a fraction of the hundreds of photographs that were sent to us, but we thank everyone who took the time and effort to help us in this way.

Josephine M. Camus
A. Clive Jermy
Barry A. Thomas

Previous page
A bird's-eye view of the crown of a tree-fern, *Dicksonia antarctica*.

A crozier lying across part of an unfurled frond of *Cnemidaria horrida*, a tree-fern of the American tropics. The sori, groups of sporangia, are borne close to the margin of the frond segments.

Part of a frond of a maidenhair fern, *Adiantum*, showing the mature sporangia pushing up the membranous flap (*indusium*) that protected them in the early stages of development.

Ferns and related plants are found all over the world, from sea-level to high mountains. They are descended from some of the oldest plants of the earth's history, being found as fossils dating back nearly 400 million years. Although most are found in the rain forests, both tropical and temperate, their habitats range from sea-sprayed cliffs through freshwater rivers and lakes to the semi-deserts of arid climates. Just a few examples of the 1200 different species are shown in the following pages, with glimpses of their varied life-styles, habitats and usefulness to man.

Man has long been familiar with the knowledge that most conspicuous plants have flowers that, after pollination by wind or insects, produce seeds which are often tasty to eat. For many centuries, the reproduction of ferns and related plants was a complete mystery because they do not have flowers. The problem of the absence of flowers was solved by the belief that ferns produced very minute, invisible, short-lived flowers during midsummer's eve, a night credited from the time of the prehistoric Druid religion in northern Europe with mystical powers. The 'seed' was thus naturally invisible at first, and became visible only as time passed. This 'seed' is now known to be the spores, each a dust-like cell so small that 25 lined up just equal a millimetre in length. It was late in the eighteenth century before the basic details of the complicated reproductive process were known.

The leaves, or fronds, of ferns span an amazing range of shapes and sizes, and their diversity is illustrated throughout this book. Some are undivided, others are so finely dissected that they resemble lace; and they range in length from a few millimetres to over seven metres long. All but the moonworts and grape ferns have fronds that, in the bud stage, are tightly coiled into the familiar fern crozier that is usually protected by a covering of scales or hairs. The first fronds to appear in a new season's growth are purely vegetative; fronds unfurling later have the *sporangia* (spore capsules). Sporangia-bearing fronds may be otherwise identical to vegetative fronds, or may have narrow *pinnae* (leaf segments) that do not extend beyond the sporangial zone. Sometimes only part of the frond is fertile.

Sporangia form on the underside of the frond, being pale at first and darkening as the spores mature within them. The sporangia are usually arranged in finite patches (*sori*) that lie along veins or over vein endings. Sori may be scattered over the lower pinna surface or occur only at the margin. They may be linear, curved, oval or round. In many ferns, each sorus is protected at least in the early stages of development by membranous tissue called an *indusium*, whilst others have evolved a cup-like structure to enclose the sorus. The sori of other genera lack any protection and are often described as naked.

The great majority of ferns have sporangia that are stalked capsules with walls only one cell thick. This wall is composed of different types of cells, the most obvious of which is a row of thickened cells that act almost like a spring as the sporangium matures and dries out, causing the sporangium to rip wide apart. The spores are forcefully flung out as the upper part of the sporangium immediately flicks backs, almost closing the capsule again. Details of the sorus, indusium, sporangium and spores are used, together with the dissection of the fronds and the anatomy of the whole plant, to distinguish the many different kinds of

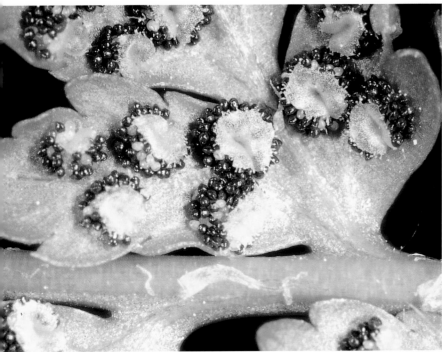

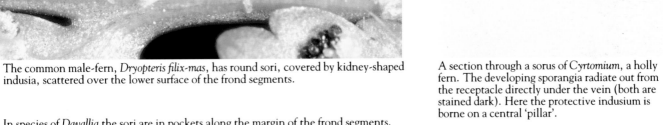

The common male-fern, *Dryopteris filix-mas*, has round sori, covered by kidney-shaped indusia, scattered over the lower surface of the frond segments.

In species of *Davallia* the sori are in pockets along the margin of the frond segments. Golden sporangia are protruding from the mouths of the pockets.

A section through a sorus of *Cyrtomium*, a holly fern. The developing sporangia radiate out from the receptacle directly under the vein (both are stained dark). Here the protective indusium is borne on a central 'pillar'.

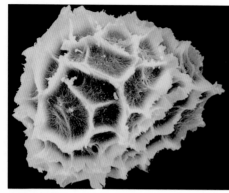

A spore of *Psomiocarpa apiifolia* with an elaborate outer layer.

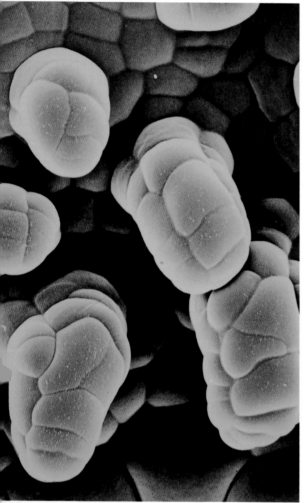

Necks of archegonia, the reproductive structures that each contain one egg-cell, protruding from the lower surface of a bracken prothallus.

An antheridium, the reproductive structure that produces sperm, on the lower surface of a bracken prothallus.

ferns and group them into an ascending hierarchy of species, genera, families and orders.

Most ferns of the order Filicales have 64 spores in each sporangium, though some have as few as 32 or 16. Ferns of the orders Ophioglossales and Marattiales have several thousand. Ovoid spores are common, but some species produce spherical ones. The surface of spores is often highly decorated, and the pattern of flanges, wings or spines may be diagnostic of a species. They may be carried only a few centimetres or several hundred kilometres by air currents. If they settle on a suitably damp surface, they germinate to produce a tongue of cells that in most ferns soon develops into an approximately heart-shaped pad of delicate green tissue called a *prothallus* or *gametophyte*. This tiny plant, less than 1 cm long, has root-like hairs called rhizoids to anchor it to soil, bark or rock. It lives in the same way as the much more conspicuous plant that produced the spores by absorbing water-borne minerals through the rhizoids and using the energy of sunlight to make its food substances (photosynthesis). The prothallus is several cells thick in the centre, but only one cell thick elsewhere. The reproductive organs, *antheridia* and *archegonia*, develop on its lower surface. Numerous *antherozoids* (sperm) are produced in the antheridia and they swim through the covering film of water to reach the archegonia, each of which contains a single egg cell. Antheridia are formed before the archegonia to increase the chance of fertilization between different prothalli and so keep a high level of potential genetic variation. This also gives the possibility of fertilization by sperm from another species of the same genus, with the result that a hybrid fern is formed. Such a fern generally produces imperfect spores and therefore cannot reproduce sexually. Recent studies of chromosomes in several genera of ferns have shown that their evolutionary history is a complicated network of hybridization. The first sporeling leaves to appear are very simple and often quite unlike the fronds characteristic of the mature fern. Successive leaves show a sequential modification until the final degree of dissection and architecture has been reached. Studying this progressive change can be helpful in working out the relationships between species of a genus.

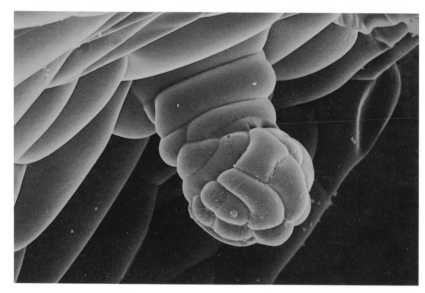

Some prothalli, like this one of a species of ribbon fern (*Vittaria minima*), produce clusters of cells called gemmae which break off to form new prothalli.

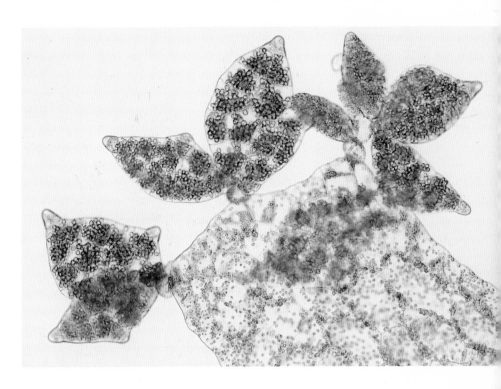

A classically heart-shaped fern prothallus or gametophyte.

A sporeling fern, still attached to the now redundant prothallus, showing sequential changes in leaves from juvenile stages towards the adult frond form.

The fertile zone of a clubmoss (*Lycopodium* species) showing the sporangia at the base of the leaves.

All ferns and their more primitive relatives have basically the same method of sexual reproduction taking place in a free-living gameto-phyte. The clubmosses, quillworts and horsetails are a rather curious assemblage of plants. They are traditionally grouped with ferns because they are more closely related to that group than to any other group of living plants. Clubmosses and quillworts differ from ferns in one very marked respect: they only have one sporangium per leaf, and this is always at the base of the leaf. Whilst the sporangia-bearing leaves (*sporophylls*) of some clubmosses are borne in a terminal spike, others have less conspicuous zones of sporophylls and vegetative leaves alternating along the stem. Quillworts, members of the genus *Isoetes*, grow at the bottom of mountain lakes or on seasonally damp land. Their presence is often overlooked because, as the illustrations later in the book show, they are easily mistaken for vegetative states of other aquatic plants. Some clubmosses, which are often all grouped in the one genus *Lycopodium*, produce spores which form bisexual prothalli as in the ferns. Quillworts and other clubmosses (*Selaginella*) bear two sorts of sporangia, containing either large or small spores which germinate to give female or male gametophytes respectively.

All species of horsetails belong to the genus *Equisetum*. They often form conspicuous stands in damp or wet places. One common species, *Equisetum arvense*, is cursed by many gardeners for its invasiveness. Although many horsetails look feathery, this effect is due to the whorled arrangement of the branches on the main stem rather than to the leaves which are vestigial, papery and fused into a sheath round the nodes of the stem. The sporangia of horsetails are produced at the margins of polygonal structures called *sporangiophores* which are grouped into a 'cone'. The cones are borne typically at the apex of the main shoot, but on the branch apices in some species. One group of horsetails produces the 'cone' on a very bizarre-looking, pale shoot that dies once the spores have been shed. The green vegetative shoots grow later. Spores are green and have four 'arms' (*elators*) that twist about when the humidity of the air changes, and it is this movement that helps to disperse them away from the parent plant.

The 'cones' of *Equisetum arvense*, a common horsetail. The polygonal sporangiophores each bear many sporangia.

Vegetative shoots of *Equisetum arvense*, showing ▷ the whorled branches.

A bulbil of a clubmoss (*Lycopodium*). This plantlet is easily dislodged from the parent plant and can quickly grow into a full plant.

Some ferns, clubmosses and horsetails form large colonies from creeping stems. A single plant of bracken can cover a whole hillside. Attractive house and garden plants are often propagated from cuttings that are nurtured to produce roots. This is a way of increasing the population without sexual reproduction, and many plants are naturally able to produce such clones of themselves. A trampled horsetail will readily break up into fragments which can develop roots and establish themselves as new plants. If the fragments are swept away by a stream or river and settle elsewhere, a new population is formed. Some clubmosses produce small plantlets called bulbils on mini-branches between the leaves. These are easily dislodged by gusts of wind or passing animals and, if they land in a suitable place, quickly grow into a full plant. Some ferns also produce bulbils, either along the frond midrib or at the tip of a frond that arches over and touches the ground. These are less easily dislodged than those of clubmosses and may have to wait until the parent frond dies before they can become established as separate plants.

Bulbils at different stages of development on the frond of *Diplazium proliferum*.

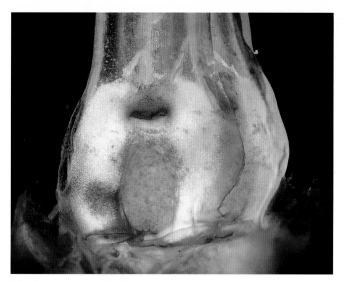

The base of a fertile leaf of a quillwort, *Isoetes echinospora*, showing the sporangium bulging with megaspores.

Part of the fertile frond of a climbing fern, *Lygodium*. Sporangia are borne on the little 'tassels' on the margins of the frond segments.

The pale fertile stems of the horsetail *Equisetum arvense* emerge in spring and die before the green vegetative ones appear.

Previous page
Rooting bases of giant clubmosses excavated from a quarry, Victoria Park, Glasgow, Scotland.

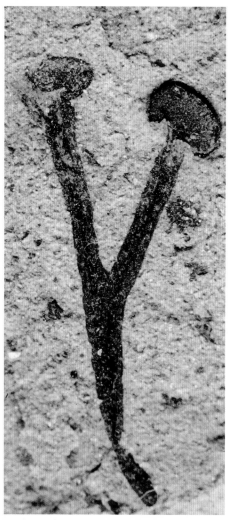

Cooksonia pertonii, one of the earliest pteridophyte-like plants from the Late Silurian, 415 million years ago, of the Welsh borderland. The specimen is only just over 1 cm tall.

Life has existed on Earth for over 3000 million years, although for most of this time it was restricted to the oceans of the world. It was only about 400 million years ago that the first multicellular plants left the water to invade the much more hostile environments on land. Here they had to contend with extremes of temperature, widescale run-off of water and erosion of the land surface, dust storms and periods of drought. However, in spite of all this, plant life not only managed to survive out of the water, but rapidly spread over the barren land.

The first of these land plants were simple dichotomising stems, just over a centimetre tall, that terminated in sporangia. Nevertheless they had all the necessary adaptations for survival, including the important central vascular strand of specialized cells for water and food conduction, and a covering of desiccation-resistant cuticle perforated by stomata, specialized structures that allow the exchange of oxygen and carbon dioxide between plant and air. Such plants were in essence pteridophytes, although they are classified in the extinct group known as the Psilophytes. They spread along the shores and coastal river banks of the late Silurian and early Devonian continent that was composed of parts of the then adjacent North America and Europe. Their simple genetic make-up and a virtual lack of competition for new habitats stimulated a very rapid series of evolutionary changes that initiated the beginnings of the plant groups that exist today. Within a little over 100 million years, there were recognizable members of nearly all the living major groups of vascular plants – ferns, horsetails, lycopsids, cycads, maidenhair trees and conifers. Indisputable flowering plants have not been found as fossils older than about 125 million years, although certain palm-like fossils suggest that they evolved much earlier.

The remains of plants are recognizable in rocks as fossils and it is from studying these fragmentary pieces of evidence that palaeobotanists reconstruct long-extinct plants and interpret their evolutionary histories and taxonomic interrelationships. Fossils also provide the means of piecing together information for our ideas of past floras and local ecologies, and for dating rocks of previously unknown or of uncertain age.

The interpretation of plant fossils may sound fairly simple and straightforward, but it is not, as fossils are very rarely whole plants. Instead they are either organs that were shed, or torn, from living plants, or fragments of dead and possibly decaying ones. Fossilization itself also depends upon the chance deposition of the plant remains into an environment suitable for preservation and incorporation into accumulating sediments. The length of time that this takes controls the amount of decay that may occur before preservation, and the remains available for study are, therefore, usually only imperfectly preserved fragments of plants. Furthermore, it is chance, again, that usually determines the collection of fossils for preservation and study. The fossil record can thus be only very limited in extent and represents only a tiny fraction of the different types of plants that once grew on Earth. Nevertheless, after 170 years of palaeobotanical study, it is one which permits us to have some overall understanding of the evolutionary history of ferns and their allies.

Fern-like ancestors appear to have evolved in many ways to form the great range of those plants we now call ferns. Most living ferns have

Psalixochlaena, a typical Carboniferous, approximately 300 million year old, early 'fern' showing the beautifully preserved cellular anatomy of its 1 cm broad frond stem and smaller frond rachis preserved in a mixture of calcium and magnesium carbonate.

large leaves, often called fronds, with well-developed vascular systems and sporangia on their undersides. The fern-like ancestors show a range of characters which permit them to be artificially grouped into three families or classes, but they are all without flattened leaves and all have unusual vascular systems. Many of them are known only from fragments that have been preserved as *permineralizations*, where the plant tissue was infiltrated with mineral-rich water that permeated the cells with a mineral matrix. This mode of preservation retains more information of the original plant than any other, but sectioning techniques are required to interpret them.

About 300 million years ago, the Carboniferous Coal Measures swamps were home to the largest pteridophytes that have ever lived. Here, in the extensive swamps, 45 metre-tall clubmosses periodically formed vast areas of closed forests, while the river banks and ox-bow lakes were often fringed with impenetrable thickets of giant horsetails. Ferns and the outwardly similar seed-ferns (now considered to be gymnosperms) were abundant in the swamps and on the river levees. Such Coal Measures ferns were often preserved as compressions, when their remains were entombed in rapidly accumulating fine grained

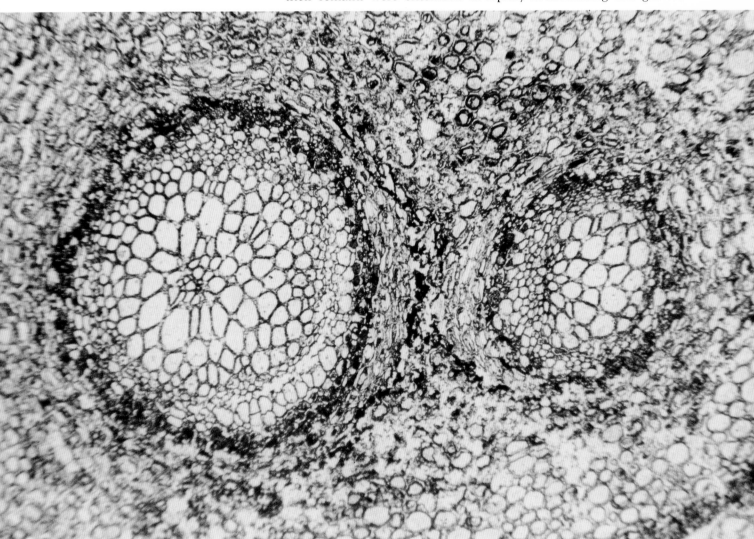

Senftenbergia, a 25 cm long portion of a compression of an approximately 300 million year old fertile schizaeaceous-like fern from the British Coal Measures.

Psaronius, a polished section of a 260 million year old permineralized Permian marattialean tree-fern trunk from France.

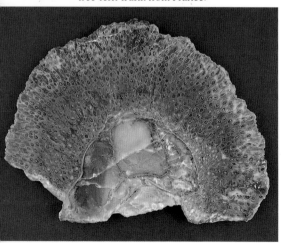

sediments where the anaerobic conditions prevented decay. Consolidation of the plant tissues through a softening of the cell walls and a collapse of internal cell spaces then accompanied the compaction of the sediments. Finally, the plant residues became coalified as the sediments turned to shale or sandstone through lithification. Splitting rocks containing such fossils often yields one coalified part, the *compression*, and an *impression counterpart* on the other. The compressions often show details of their sporangia and their spatial arrangements on the frond. Acidic oxidation of these sporangia can often liberate the remains of the spores and their resistant outer layers often reveal great details in ornamentation. Similarly acidic oxidation of coal and shales can liberate large numbers of spores that were preserved after liberation from their parent plants.

Some Coal Measures ferns were relatively small. One of these, *Senftenbergia*, has very similar sporangia to those of living schizaeaceous ferns and was for some time thought to belong to this group. Others, such as *Psaronius*, were as large, if not larger, than living tree-ferns, to which, however, they are unrelated being instead ancestral forms of the living marattialean tropical ferns such as *Marattia* and *Angiopteris*. As they were so large, it is unusual to find other than small fragments of their leaves preserved as coalified compressions. Very occasionally growth stages, such as croziers, can be found. Their stems, being much stronger, can often be found as large pieces preserved as either compressions, impressions, permineralizations or as three-dimensional *casts*.

Large plants such as these highlight the difficulty of naming separated and dispersed plant organs. The stems are known as *Psaronius* when permineralized, but are called *Caulopteris* or *Megaphyton* if preserved as compressions. The fronds may be called *Pecopteris* or *Cyathocarpus* when found as compressions or *Scolecopteris* or *Asterotheca* if permineralised. The spores are called *Punctatisporites* when found dispersed from the parent fructification. Such a multiplicity of names may seem unnecessary or even ridiculous, but the system is one which provides a workable means of naming specimens in an understandable way that also describes their mode of preservation.

The Osmundales, which includes the living Royal Fern *Osmunda regalis*, evolved about 280 million years ago in the more northern and colder environments of the Permian that followed the demise of the Coal Measures swamps. They rapidly diversified indicating a high rate of evolutionary change, but the group quickly went into decline, to leave only the 16 species in three genera alive today.

Lobatopteris miltonii, a portion of a *c.* 300 million year old sterile marattialean frond from the Coal Measures of Switzerland. This compression has been completely replaced by a structureless chloritic mineral.

Lobatopteris miltonii, a portion of a *c.* 300 million year old sterile marattialean frond from the British Coal Measures. The black compression stands out clearly against the grey shale.

Asterotheca miltonii, a portion of a *c.* 300 million year old fertile marattialean frond from the Coal Measures of Czechoslovakia. The sandstone surrounding the fern is stained yellowish coloured by iron.

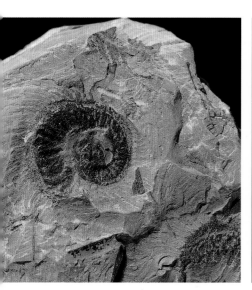

Crozier of a *c.* 300 million year old marattialean fern from the British Coal Measures.

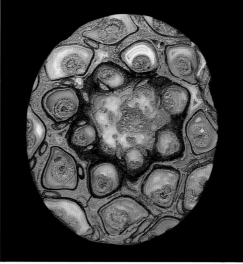

Palaeosmunda williamsii, a polished section of a 260 million year old osmundaceous tree-fern trunk from Australia. The stem with a surrounding mantle of petiole bases can be seen here preserved in chalcedony.

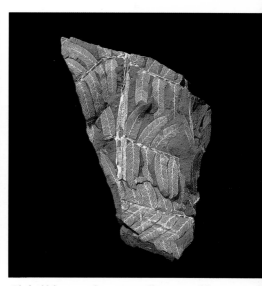

Cladophlebis australis, a 260 million year old osmundaceous leaf from the Permian of Australia. The axes and veins have been replaced by white kaolinite.

Arnophyton kuesii, a 280 million year old fern-like plant from the Lower Permian of New Mexico, USA. This small, almost complete plant shows both juvenile and less dissected adult fronds.

There is one unusual fern-like plant known from the Permian of New Mexico which is especially worthy of mention. *Arnophyton kuesii* is a nearly complete juvenile plant having a horizontal stem with roots, a short upright aerial shoot and a tuft of leaves of two kinds representing juvenile and adult forms. As such it is the only complete juvenile fern-like plant known.

There was a great change in the world's vegetation at the start of the Mesozoic and many new plants appeared at around this time. The ferns diversified especially during the Triassic and Jurassic periods of 250–150 million years ago, and are often very abundant in fossil assemblages indicating that they were probably the dominant herbs on land. This is most likely because the clubmosses and horsetails were in decline and rare, there were few smaller gymnosperms and the flowering plants had not yet made an appearance. Plants belonging to other living fern families, such as the Schizaeaceae, Gleicheniaceae, Dipteridaceae, Matoniaceae, Cyatheaceae, Dicksoniaceae made their appearance at this time, and possibly the Polypodiaceae.

The Matoniaceae was particularly widespread at this time although the only living genus *Matonia*, which is illustrated in the chapter on Mountains, is restricted to South East Asia. The oldest fossils of this family belong to the genus *Phlebopteris* which was in fact described before the living relatives. For this reason *Matonia* is often described as a 'living fossil'.

Weichselia reticulata was a particularly successful member of the Matoniaceae, dominating communities that were subjected to periods of extreme drought. It possessed a number of xeromorphic characters in its leaves including fibrous tissue, a thick cuticle and sunken stomata. Pure assemblages of charcoalified leaf fragments of this species in southern England suggest that it grew in stands that were sometimes spontaneously burnt. The nearest modern analogy is bracken.

The Jurassic *Aspidistes* is possibly a member of the Polypodiaceae, but apart from this the earliest records of this family are from the Tertiary. It is likely that the appearance and rapid expansion of the flowering plants about 90–50 million years ago in the late Cretaceous and early Tertiary created new communities, and the evolution of new herbaceous flowering plants gave direct competition to the ferns. The extinction of many animal groups at the Cretaceous/Tertiary boundary, 65 million years ago, has also stimulated much discussion on possible climatic changes. There were vegetational changes, but not comparable widescale extinctions. One interesting feature is the presence of a fern dominated assemblage in sediments immediately above the boundary. This could be the result of ferns rapidly colonizing barren areas similar to the modern invasion of *Pityrogramma calomelanos* into volcanically devastated areas in Mexico illustrated in the chapter on Arid Zones.

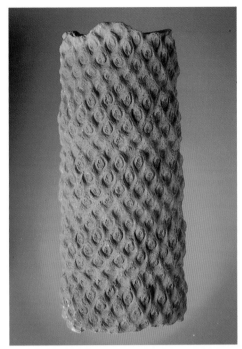

Protopteris punctata, an internal cast of a 110 million year old cyatheaceous tree-fern stem from the Lower Cretaceous of England. Wavy marks of the U-shaped vascular tissue are visible in the oval outlines of the leaf bases.

Dicksonia mariopteris, a 170 million year old dicksoniaceous fern frond from the Jurassic of Yorkshire, UK.

Phlebopteris smithii, a 220 million year old matoniaceous fern frond from the Triassic of New Mexico, USA. The typical palmate arrangement of the frond is clearly visible.

Weichselia reticulata, 150 million year old charcoal remains of burnt fronds are strewn over the surface of this fine-grained siltstone from the British Cretaceous of the Isle of Wight.

Azolla, 40 million year old plants from the Tertiary of Canada showing a length of the floating stem with its long dangling roots.

The development of different types of vegetation seems then to have stimulated a new evolutionary burst in the ferns giving rise to forms directly referable to modern genera. The water-ferns, *Salvinia* and *Azolla,* are known from Tertiary deposits as are specimens showing a remarkable resemblance to the widely distributed North American grape fern, *Botrychium virginianum.* Unfortunately, reliable records of polypodiaceous ferns are very few. There are Canadian specimens which are virtually indistinguishable from the sensitive fern, *Onoclea sensibilis,* that grows today in a wide range of localities throughout North America. Other records of polypodiaceous ferns are limited to fertile fragments of the coastal dwelling *Acrostichum,* anatomically preserved rhizomes and frond rachises that belong to the Dennstaedtiaceae and a number of sterile foliage fragments that cannot be reliably named. The general paucity of polypodiaceous ferns most probably reflects a growth pattern where fronds rapidly collapse, wilt and die on the plants. Even so, some became fossilized so further discoveries should continue to increase our knowledge and understanding of their evolutionary history.

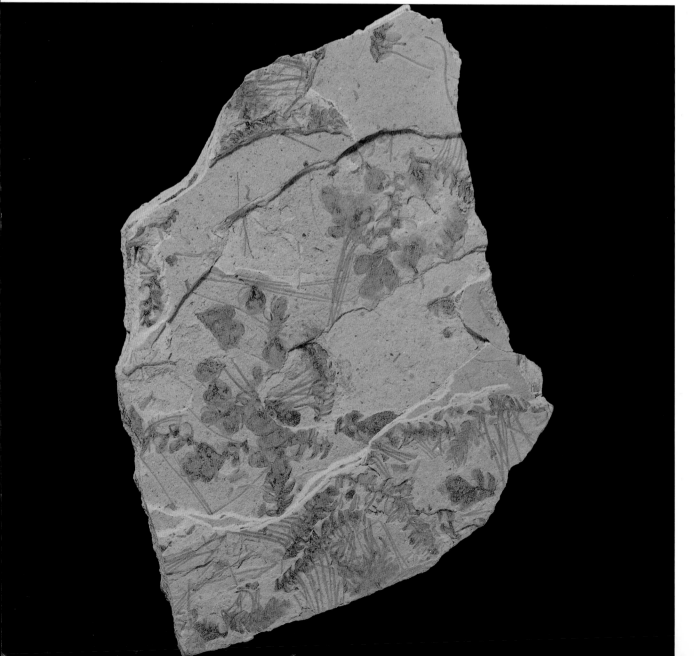

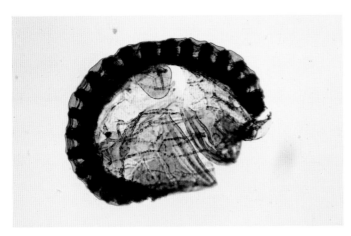

Acrostichum anglicum, a 36 million year old dispersed sporangium containing one residual spore from the British Tertiary of the Isle of Wight.

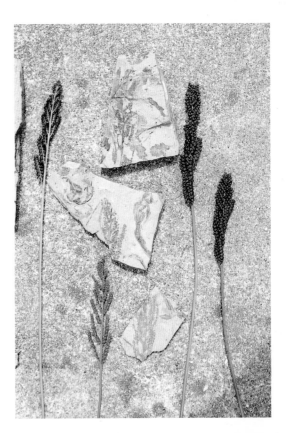

Onoclea sensibilis, a 40 million year old fern from the early Tertiary of Alberta, Canada showing (*right*) the very reduced fertile frond with clusters of sporangia, and (*below*) the broader sterile frond. There are no discernible differences between the fossil and living plants, so they are given the same name.

TROPICAL FORESTS

Previous page
Lowland dipterocarp forest on the limestone hills of Gunung Mulu National Park, Sarawak.

A low tree in the seasonally dry forest in Malaysia bearing the epiphytic bird's nest ferns, *Asplenium nidus* and *Microsorum punctatum*.

An epiphytic bracket fern (*Merinthosorus*) on the branches of a fallen forest giant on the lower slopes of Mt Kinabalu, Sabah.

The narrow girdle of the tropics around the Earth's equator gives us the exotic atolls, savannahs and rain forests. Here the day-length changes only slightly, if at all, and temperatures vary, not with seasons, but only with altitude. Vegetation and animals alike must be adapted, not to those cold darkening days of winter, but to changing regimes of rainfall, brought about by rain-bearing trade winds. The climax vegetation here, like elsewhere, is forest, and it is in these humid tropical jungles of the world – or rain forests, as they are more technically called – that ferns develop both in luxuriance and diversity. A quarter of our world lies between the Tropics of Cancer and Capricorn but only a small fraction of this equatorial belt supports rain forest.

Some areas will vary in the amounts of rain they receive because of the seasonal variation in the direction of trade winds. Those with a distinct and often prolonged dry period before torrential seasonal rains begin are called 'monsoon' areas, and the forests there have a less rich fern flora, albeit one which shows adaptations for combating those drier periods. Much of the forest in the Mekong valley of Vietnam, Laos and Cambodia is of this type. A similar seasonal climate is found in parts of Indonesia, stretching from Sumatra to Irian Jaya, and in the southern part of Papua New Guinea, areas which are also shadowed from one or other of the trade winds. Trees in monsoon forests do not grow so close together as in rain forests and the land is more easily cleared for agriculture, with rice being the usual crop. The larger trees, however, may be covered in many epiphytes – plants that grow upon other plants, but which do not tap the host's food resources as a parasite like mistletoe does. These include ferns such as the stag's horn (*Platycerium*) and an assortment of bracket ferns (*Aglaomorpha, Drynaria* and *Merinthosorus*). In Africa much of the tropical belt is covered by a similar drier forest or thorn scrub in which seasonal drought plays a significant part in the life-cycle of the ferns found there. These are described in the chapter on Arid Zones.

In other areas these rain-bearing winds may follow each other, coming first from one direction, then from another, and the climate is continually wet. In such warm, humid regions develop the most luxuriant forests of all – the tropical rain forests. It is deep in these tropical rain forests that life is easiest for ferns and their relatives. In the lowlands, protected by trees 30–40 metres or more tall, and in the mountain forests frequently bathed in cloud and mist, ferns flourish and show their greatest diversity of leaf form to exploit every possible niche. All that has been written, and is now being said, about tropical rain forests and the unknown riches they contain, relates to ferns and clubmosses as much as it does to palms, lianas and forest trees. The numbers of genera and species increase ten-fold from those we can see in more temperate lands, and there are a number of other reasons for this in addition to the abundant water. Firstly, the tropical latitudes enjoy a higher average temperature, at least in their lower altitudes, while even high on mountains the tropical sun blazes down through the rarefied air to heat any bare rock surface to a temperature sufficient to fry an egg. The chapter on Mountain Summits illustrates the need for adaptations against the contrasting cold nights. Secondly, the range of natural habitats is considerable – from swamps and lakes, through mixed

Miombo woodland in eastern Zambia, habitat of terrestrial species of lesser clubmosses (*Selaginella*) and cloak ferns (*Cheilanthes*).

Mohria lepigera, a fern frequently found in the high rainfall woodland of the granite hills in central Zimbabwe.

grassland with scrub and trees, to primeval forest of various kinds depending on soils, topography and altitude. In places – and there are many – where man has cleared land to build dwellings and to grow crops, ferns quickly fill any suitable niches and cover roadside banks, old garden plots and worked-over forest.

Rain forests are found in all continents within the tropical belt. The largest expanse of jungle lies in the vast Amazon basin of South America, rising in the west to form mist forests on the middle slopes of the Andes. As one would expect, the seaward slopes facing the Pacific (in Colombia and Ecuador) are also rich in these forests, with probably the most diverse flora and fauna in all the world. In Central America good forests have developed in Panama and Costa Rica, through Guatemala and Honduras to southern Mexico, although much has been lost to sugar-cane and fruit plantations.

Rich montane forest at 2600 metres, Pampa Tambo, Bolivia, with a fine specimen of the tree-fern, *Dicksonia sellowiana*.

The fan-leaved elephant's tongue (*Elaphoglossum peltatum*) creeping on a moss-covered branchlet in mid-montane forest in Venezuela. The button-sized fertile leaf in the centre of the picture has been turned over to show the underside covered with black sporangia.

Ridge-tops in the Ecuadorian Andes are covered by elfin forest. Tree-ferns, like this *Trichipteris conjugata*, will only grow above the surrounding canopy where the clouds are frequently low enough to shroud them in mist.

Left
The hand fern (*Cheiroglossa palmata*) grows mainly in lowland forest of the Americas, but sometimes at an altitude of 2300 metres, as here in Bolivia. It is an epiphytic adder's tongue found as far north as southern Florida, USA, and also on Madagascar and Île de Réunion.

Right
A vividly coloured filmy fern (*Sphaerocionium* species) on a tree trunk in a fairly open glade in the mist forest at 2500 metres in Bolivia.

Mid-montane forest areas where the topography is more gentle, such as here on Île de Réunion, are often cleared, first for firewood and then hill cultivation.

In the darker montane rain forest, trunks of larger trees may be festooned with small polypodies and finger ferns. This example of the latter *Xiphopteris villosissima*, is found on Mt Mulanje, Malawi.

In Africa wet rain forest is found in the Zaïre River basin, through Cameroon to an important strip along the West African coast to Guinea. The isolated patches that occur in East Africa are on mountains such as the Usambara Mountains in Tanzania. Madagascar, once rich in tropical forest, has only a few remaining remnants which are still remarkably rich in numbers of unique species and therefore vital to conserve. Only relatively few isolated tropical islands have the rain forest habitat. These include Réunion in the Indian Ocean, and New Caledonia, Fiji, the Marquesas and Hawaiian Islands in the Pacific.

The many islands of Indonesia and Malaysia and the nearby continental lands of Australia (Queensland), South East Asia and India were once clothed in rain forest, but the lowland forest has been felled in most of this region, with only a few areas left in Laos, Vietnam, Thailand and Burma. Mountain chains running from the Himalayas, through Malaysia and the Indonesian archipelago, to Papua New Guinea, increase the altitudinal variation to give a range of montane forest types. Each of these is rich in ferns, and safe for the time being from commercial exploitation because they are mostly on steep slopes. In India, there is a small amount of montane rain forest in the Eastern and Western Ghats, the Nilgiri Hills have ever-wet rain forest and an appreciable amount remains in Sri Lanka.

The most important timber trees in the constantly wet lowland rain forest of Borneo are those of the Dipterocarpaceae family which includes the Philippine mahogany and Malaysian *meranti*. Trees in this family also help to shape the structure of the rain forest, containing some of the largest, often reaching over 50 metres. Some species rise high above other forest trees and their enormous crowns and large branches are home to a variety of ferns and clubmosses, orchids and screw-pines. Living over 30 metres from the ground could have its problems. For instance, how far do roots have to go to get water and nutrients? In this very wet climate it rains almost every day and acquiring water proves no problem. However, if the sensitive water-absorbing rootlets of the plant are to remain active they must be protected from those dry periods between the showers. Many large epiphytes, like the bird's nest fern, *Asplenium nidus*, form a highly branched, wiry root system that protects the finer roots and at the same time holds water as would an absorbent sponge. Other species, like the bracket ferns, *Aglaomorpha heraclea* and species of *Drynaria*, take this one stage further, and have very tough basal leaves that are not shed when they die, but form a basket to contain the roots of each fern. When the more normal leaves on the plant die, they and those from the surrounding branches of the host tree are trapped in the basket, and soon rot down to form a natural compost, providing the fern with all the nutrients it needs – recycled from their own waste!

Few ferns equal the height or leaf-length of this elephant fern (*Angiopteris* species) ▷ in lowland forest of eastern Papua New Guinea.

An epiphytic species of clubmoss, *Lycopodium phyllicifolium*, in mid-montane forest in Ecuador.

A rocky stream in Gunung Mulu National Park, Sarawak, with a young plant of the elephant fern (*Angiopteris* species), a common species in the lower montane rain forest.

Opposite
A few species of clubmoss climb, or more correctly scramble, over shrubs in ridge or secondary vegetation. Here the slender tassled branches of *Lycopodium casuarinoides* are seen hanging from saplings in the *Dacrydium* forest at 3300 metres on Mt Kinabalu, Sabah.

Other epiphytic plants colonize this rich, spongy root mat which is soon festooned with ferns such as the ribbon fern (a pendulous adder's tongue, *Ophioglossum pendulum*), and bootlace ferns (*Vittaria*) as well as orchids, peperomias and clubmosses (*Lycopodium* species). Furthermore, ants, which abound in the tropical forest, also invade these lofty habitats, adding their quota of organic and inorganic particles to the compost. This mini ecosystem is so complete that one even finds earthworms enjoying the humus of an aerial garden.

Almost every pteridophyte family has genera or species adapted to the epiphytic habit. Some, like the majority of *Grammitis* species, *Vaginularia* and the fingernail-sized *Microgonium* species, are very small, and grow among the mossy tufts on branches in the mist forests and on the finer twigs of the large lowland canopies. Others, such as the hare's foot ferns (*Davallia*), may have fronds a metre or more long, while the elephant's tongues (*Elaphoglossum*) can form large clumps, hanging upside down on a horizontal branch. The bird's nest ferns, *Asplenium nidus* in South East Asia and its New World counterpart *Asplenium phyllitidis*, may reach massive proportions with a single plant weighing over 100 kilograms, while its rootmass amazingly balances on the most slender of branches. Other characteristic epiphytes on the larger trunks are species of *Lycopodium* known as tassel ferns, which as in *Lycopodium phlegmaria*, for example, may be like a hanging form of the fir clubmoss of northern mountains. Another species, *Lycopodium pinifolium*, is aptly named through its resemblance to a needle-bearing fir tree branch.

Opposite
The erect climbing rhizome of *Teratophyllum aculeatum*, firmly attached to the trunk of a tree where it produces fertile leaves high in the forest canopy in Borneo. The sporangia are not grouped into distinct sori but cover the entire under-surface of the leaflet, as in the elephant's tongue, *Elaphoglossum*.

These fronds of *Teratophyllum aculeatum* rising from slender, far-creeping rhizomes may be found covering considerable areas of the forest floor in lowland dipterocarp forest in Borneo. They are never fertile and are quite different from those formed when the rhizome climbs to lighter areas in the forest canopy.

Some plants have evolved slender, flexible stems (rhizomes) that twine round trunks or branches. In this way, many ferns climb the most slender sapling in the lowland alluvial forest, and *Stenochlaena palustris* is able to worm its way through the spiny armour of the forest palms. Some species, especially those in the family Lomariopsidaceae, begin life on the forest floor where the rhizomes, creeping over the ground, bear leaves different both in shape and texture from the aerial ones produced later. These first leaves are never fertile and may dominate areas of the forest floor while their rhizomes find a trunk to climb high into the canopy. In contrast to the slender, creeping rhizomes on the ground, those climbing the tree are thick, with sucker-like rootlets, and produce large compound leaves that will eventually bear spores.

The rhizomes of some epiphytic ferns are thick and fleshy, storing food and water against the periods of adverse conditions met with in monsoon forests, where several months without rain can be normal. Most members of the polypody family have a zone on their leaf-stalk which can die off quickly to effect a natural break causing the leaf (or leaflet) to fall, just as leaves of deciduous trees do in winter. This again is an adaptation to prevent the fern losing too much water through its leaf pores. Other ferns characteristic of these forests have evolved different ways to cope with this problem. The felt ferns (*Pyrrosia*) have a welt of star-shaped hairs covering the leaf which itself can curl up to prevent further water loss. This feature is discussed further in the chapter on Arid Zones.

In the constantly wet rain forest, polypods with thick fleshy rhizomes have developed a curious life-style: the central pith cells of the rhizome lose their sap and shrink on aging, and the older parts of the rhizome become hollow. These hollow stems are explored by ants, first for food and then as a nest site in which to rear young. The fern, in exchange for this free housing, is guarded by the ants against attacks from other insect herbivores. The ants also bring a source of nitrogen – that important element for growth – to the host plant, through their faeces (droppings) and frass from food brought to larvae. One genus of tropical Asian polypodies, *Lecanopteris*, has evolved a number of species all of which are ant-plants. This is paralleled, as is often the case in such specialized evolution, by a New World equivalent: the potato fern (*Solanopteris brunei*) of Costa Rica and northern South America has a potato-like tuberous rhizome which ants also colonize.

In tropical mountains, forests above 1200 metres are usually in a zone that is enshrouded in cloud for part of the day. Some saddles on the mountain ridges are particularly rich in ferns because the mist rarely clears. Such a habitat is known as montane forest, and the lower branches of the tropical oaks and chestnuts growing here sport an abundance of rat-tail polypodies (*Belvisia* species) and other genera in

Mossy forest at 2000 metres in Seram, ▷
Moluccas, Indonesia.

An ant-fern (*Lecanopteris carnosa*) showing the succulent branched rhizome which is inhabited by ants. This species is an epiphyte in lowland or ridge forest in SE Asia.

The fat succulent rhizomes of ant-ferns would make a tasty meal for large herbivores, including monkeys, but this species from Sulawesi, *Lecanopteris spinosa*, has spines and soon becomes tough and unattractive to foraging animals.

this varied family (*Crypsinus, Goniophlebium, Microsorum* and *Selliguea* – to name but a few). These ferns frequently cover fallen trees and, in more open patches, spread onto the forest floor. Filmy ferns are plentiful, often growing inter-mixed with mosses and liverworts, and colonizing rock or soil newly bared by streamlets. In this mist zone are also many species of tree-fern, the bright green crowns of which stand out in the canopy when seen from above. Tree-ferns, which are unable to form new growing points if the apex of the trunk is damaged, have a rough stem, scarred with leaf-stalk bases, which is ideal for epiphyte colonization. Epiphytes could, however, damage unfurling fronds and the stem apex, but this is prevented in some species of tree-fern which retain their dead leaves as a curtain around their upper trunk, giving an unstable substrate for any trespassing rhizome.

A lesser clubmoss, *Selaginella involvens*, showing the flat, leaf-like 'fronds' spreading over a rock surface in mid-montane forest on Mt Kinabalu, Sabah.

Mist forest at 2900 metres on Volcan Barva, Costa Rica. The ever-present water ▷ vapour encourages the growth of mosses and liverworts in this community (hence the name 'mossy forest'). The tree canopy here is relatively low.

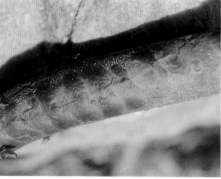

The discoid leaves of a membranous filmy fern, *Microgonium omphaloides*, adpressed to a small branch in lowland forest in New Ireland, Papua New Guinea.

An unfurling crozier of a species of *Thelypteris* from the upper montane forest of Mt Kinabalu, Sabah. The vulnerable young tissue is covered in mucus and the plant pushes out breathing organs (aerophores), seen here as long white protuberances, in order to exchange gases with the air.

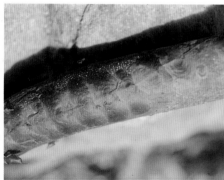

A filmy fern (*Sphaerocionium* species) making a nice display on a fallen branch in a Colombian montane forest.

Tree-ferns are seen again, often in some quantity, especially in South East Asia, in the grasslands of the higher mountains, where montane forest and the tropical bilberry and rhododendron scrub has been burnt, either by natural fires started by lightening, or by local people flushing out small animals for the pot. Such is the diversity of the tree-fern genus, *Cyathea*, that almost every mountain group has its own particular species.

These small leaves resemble a filmy fern but are really the forest floor leaves (bathyphylls) of the climbing fern, *Teratophyllum clemensiae*, seen here in Gunung Mulu National Park, Sarawak.

Some ferns, like this hard fern of the *Blechnum capense* group growing on a hillside in Sulawesi, can withstand the frequent fires in mountain grasslands.

Stunted woodland on sandy clays in Zimbabwe. Five species of adder's tongues (*Ophioglossum* species), a quillwort (*Isoetes abyssinica*) and a clover-leaf fern (*Marsilea*) grow within the area shown in the picture.

The upper montane forest in Papua New Guinea may give way to natural grassland as discussed in the chapter on Mountain Summits. Substantial stands of tree-ferns grow on Mount Wilhelm at the edge of the forest and in grassy glades.

Tapeinidum species in the monsoon forest of Thailand. Often the young leaves are a bronzy colour to protect them against the strong sunlight and make a fine display *en masse*.

Degraded land in Costa Rica cleared of forest for an abortive attempt to cultivate it and now covered in weed species of ferns like sword fern (*Nephrolepis*), tangle fern (*Gleichenia*) and species of lesser clubmosses (*Selaginella*).

The agricultural practice known as 'shifting cultivation' is an ancient one, especially in South East Asia. Forest is cleared to grow food, but the soils are so poor they can only produce two, or at the most three, consecutive crops. So the people move on to cut more virgin forest, leaving the former fields to revert to a tangle of weedy forest regrowth. In this *secondary* forest as it is called, ferns may become dominant, but there will not be many species. The sword fern (*Nephrolepis* species) will compete with the *alang-alang* grass and cover large areas in the lowland alluvial plains. Various brakes (*Pteris*), *Thelypteris* species and, along the stream banks the edible fern (*Diplazium esculentum*, *paku* in Malay), may be common. The latter is picked for sale at markets throughout Indonesia and Malaysia.

In the low foot-hills bamboos may take over on scrubby hillsides, but the tangle ferns (*Gleichenia* and *Dicranopteris* species) form dense thickets on the steeper banks. Higher still in the mountains, at around 1800 metres altitude, abandoned garden terraces revert to rough scrublands. Here tropical brackens (*Pteridium revolutum* and *Pteridium semihastatum*) and *Culcita villosa* are speedy colonizers, with large-stemmed *Blechnum* amongst them looking like small tree-ferns.

In these very wet climates landslips are a frequent feature on some of the steeper hillsides when, after a torrential downpour, saturated clay soils can easily slip away from shaley bedrock. Such is the rate of regrowth, however, that the hillside is soon covered, and ferns are some of the first to colonize. Besides tangle ferns, species of *Culcita*, *Dipteris* and the more weedy species of tree-fern such as *Cyathea contaminans* can form thickets. These have been discussed in the chapter on Mountain Summits.

The sword fern, *Nephrolepis exaltata*, spreading rapidly along a roadside verge in Costa Rica by means of its stolons and rhizomes.

Equisetum bogotense is the most widespread horsetail of the few found in South America, and may grow as a roadside weed as shown here in Costa Rica. *Equisetum ramosissimum* and *E. debile* are found in the same ecological niche in the Old World.

A creeping button fern (*Pyrrosia piloselloides*). The fertile leaves are longer than the sterile ones.

Village gardens have a mixture of planted fruit trees and wild species left to give shade to the crops of sweet potato or yams. These trees will have their share of epiphytes such as the creeping button ferns (*Pyrrosia* species) which may also be seen on street trees in the larger towns. In the garden, climbing ferns (species of *Lygodium*, *Oleandra* and *Lomagramma*) may be seen sporing freely in the low open canopies.

Rain forests all over the world are being cleared at such a rate that there is considerable international concern. Not only does the burning of forest add to the 'greenhouse gases' and subsequent effects on our climate, but it deprives people of their heritage – both locally, with homes destroyed as well in many cases, and globally – of the untapped, and mostly yet undiscovered, wealth of the fauna and flora. The disappearance of the rain forest on a world scale is a well-documented dilemma, with no easy solution. Basically it is the result of greed. Landowners want income for a better standard of living, governments need export revenue, while distant nations are hungry for the end products of forestry as plywood or weather-resistant window frames, or for beef from cattle grazed on the depauperate cleared land. Those nations' demands result from the increasingly high standards of living of individuals, and it is our responsibility to curtail that greed, demand less, and learn how to live in harmony with Earth and her resources.

The primitive fern ally, *Tmesipteris elongata*, an epiphyte in the subtropical forests of New Zealand and the South Pacific. Large green sporangia can be seen on the right of the picture.

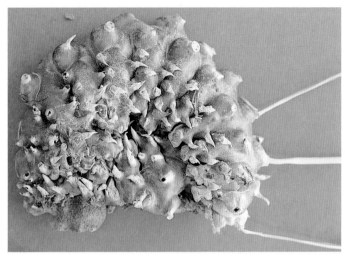

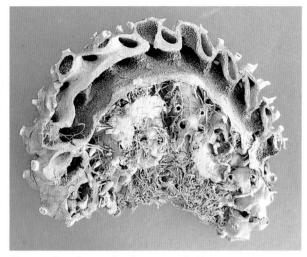

The rhizome of the ant-fern, *Lecanopteris sarcopus*, showing its succulent, but spiny, nature. Ants enter the hollow rhizome through old leaf-bases.

This ant-fern rhizome has been cut in half to show the chambers that ants colonize.

Water flows easily through the narrow leaves of this fern, *Dipteris lobbiana*, in a river-bed in Sarawak, when the river is in spate.

WETLANDS

Previous page
Eventide on Loch Awe, Scotland. The shore is dominated by the aquatic fern, pillwort (*Pilularia globulifera*), growing with the water lobelia.

The Kariba water spangles, *Salvinia molesta*, showing its potential for forming dense mats. This introduced plant reached plague proportions on Lake Kariba, Zimbabwe in the late 1950s when, as a result of vigorous growth, rafts some three metres thick were rapidly formed.

A dense stand of spring quillwort (*Isoetes echinospora*) seen on the exposed shore of a Welsh lake after an abnormally dry season.

While the greatest number and diversity of all ferns are found in the humid forests of the tropics, only relatively few are found in the wettest places, from freshwater streams and lakes to the splash zone of the seashore. The form of fern species in these habitats ranges from that of the typical fern to ones so curious that the unwitting observer would not suspect them of belonging to this group. Amongst the fern allies, the horsetails and quillworts are typical of wetlands.

The quillworts are a widespread group so similar in form that only one genus (*Isoetes*) is now recognized. In spite of this, the 100 or so species have adapted themselves to a wide range of habitats and have been illustrated also in the chapters on Mountains and Arid Zones. Some species, widely distributed around the northern hemisphere, for example *Isoetes echinospora* and *I. lacustris*, live normally totally submerged, sometimes to a depth of six metres or more. The spores of these plants, embedded at the base of the quill-like leaves may not be dispersed until an inquisitive fish disturbs the plant in search of food.

There are two free-floating genera of water ferns, the water spangles (*Salvinia*) and the mosquito ferns (*Azolla*). They have a branching growth pattern that fragments easily and enables them to spread rapidly. Both show major changes in leaf form that are obvious adaptations to life on the surface of the water and keep them not only afloat when the water is disturbed, but also floating the right way up. *Salvinia* has undivided leaves that in some species may be three cm long. The upper surface of these is typically covered with complex hairs that trap bubbles of air if the plant is submerged, enabling it to quickly right itself again. These attractive ferns are often grown in aquaria and ornamental ponds, but if they escape from these and spread beyond their natural range the consequences may be dire. This happened in 1957 when the Zambesi River in Africa was dammed at Kariba to form a reservoir for producing hydro-electric power. Within three years an alien hybrid *Salvinia*, probably from South America, came down the

A seasonal pool harbouring both a quillwort, *Isoetes*, and a clover-leaf fern, *Marsilea*, in Rajasthan, India. The hooves of the water buffalo break the ground and help spread the spores.

The Sepik River, Papua New Guinea, showing colonization by the introduced Kariba water spangles, *Salvinia molesta*. The density of this plant in the Sepik area of New Guinea is such that it prevents the use of rivers for transport

The African mosquito fern, *Azolla nilotica*. The golden reproductive organs can be seen at the bottom of the picture.

Zambesi and spread over Lake Kariba, shading out the microscopic life so important to the fish that vast numbers died, threatening the local fishing economy with collapse. Sedges and shrubs colonized the rafts of water spangles. Aptly named *Salvinia molesta*, this fern then appeared on the other side of the Indian Ocean, probably spread by migrating water birds, and has became a widespread weed of lakes and rice fields from India through South East Asia to Queensland, Australia.

The leaves of the mosquito ferns are only a couple of millimetres long, overlapping and hairless. Air is trapped between the leaves and stem and refloats the fern if it is pushed below the water surface by birds' feet, oars or the turbulence caused by boat engines. An *Azolla* from 40 million years ago is shown in the chapter on The Fossil Record. Its usefulness to man through its association with a nitrogen-fixing alga is described in Myths and Modern Uses. Two species of north temperate regions (*Azolla filiculoides* and *A. mexicana*) often turn deep red in autumn as the months of summer sunshine cause coloured chemicals called anthocyanins to build up in the leaves. In Australasia, the intensity of the sunshine is so much greater than in the temperate regions that the native species are red for the whole year. *Azolla rubra* covers small lakes in the open savannah country in Papua New Guinea, and when seen from the air gives a weird effect reminiscent of the infra-red images transmitted by some satellites scanning the earth's surface. Similar pigmentation is seen in some of the alpine clubmosses and young fronds of tropical ferns and is thought to protect leaves from the high levels of ultraviolet light.

The organs containing the sporangia of the mosquito fern, *Azolla*. The large capsule contains a single megaspore; the smaller dark sac (in the centre of the picture) contains the microspores.

Victoria Falls, Zimbabwe, where the Kariba water spangles (*Salvinia molesta*) was▷ first recorded in 1956 on the spray-covered ledges. Three years later it had spread downriver to the newly created Lake Kariba and increased rapidly after being trapped amongst the twigs of the submerged forest.

Azolla and *Salvinia*, like the quillworts (*Isoetes*) and clover-leaf ferns (*Marsilea*) described in the chapters on Mountains and Arid Zones, are also associated with water. They produce spores of two sorts (megaspores and microspores) which in these two ferns have elaborate structures to maintain buoyancy. While the stalked sori of *Azolla* are obviously associated with the underside of the leaf as in other ferns, those of *Salvinia* are borne on a root-like leaf and hang down like a row of grapes.

The clover-leaf ferns are mostly marginal swamp plants and are found throughout the world. Those from areas with a seasonal dry period have been discussed in the Arid Zones chapter. In the wet season they are well adapted to high water levels with a rapidly growing leaf-stalk bringing the four leaflets to the water surface.

The pillworts, *Pilularia*, are found in the temperate regions of the world and are related to the clover-leaf ferns although they look very different with their rush-like leaves. These leaves, however, do show the circinnate crozier characteristic of nearly all ferns. Pillwort grows on the margins and in the shallows of ponds and lakes, where it may form large colonies by its creeping rhizome. Like *Marsilea*, it produces a hard structure called a sporocarp that can survive several years of drought and only splits open in wet conditions to release a mucilaginous mass containing both mega- and microsporangia.

Another less attractive water fern has been given the charming name of water sprite. *Ceratopteris thalictroides* is native to South East Asia where, until the advent of herbicides, it was a common weed of rice fields. It grows in full sun in ditches and shallow ponds, and is still eaten as a vegetable. Though other species of the same genus are entirely floating, buoyed up by their spongy leaf-stalks, this fern is rooted in mud with the fleshy fronds protruding from the water. The fertile fronds are

Floating leaves of the clover-leaf fern, *Marsilea strigosa*, in a pool in southern France.

A heathland pool in the the New Forest, southern England, with an apple-green sward of pillwort, *Pilularia globulifera*. Habitats for this species are becoming scarce as heathland is drained and converted to forest plantation.

A closer view of pillwort (*Pilularia globulifera*) showing the rush-like leaves and the spore-bearing organs – the 'pills'. These are borne directly on the rhizome and are highly modified leaves.

The dehisced 'pills' of the pillwort, exposing the larger (white) megaspores and the smaller, more numerous, microspores embedded in a natural nutritive jelly produced by the 'pill' wall and in which the next stage of the life-cycle will take place.

The water sprite, *Ceratopteris thalictroides*, in a marginal swamp in a Malaysian village. Note the plastic sandal brought along in the last rainstorm. Most of the leaves seen are fertile ones with narrow segments; later, vegetative leaves will be formed – and most likely collected for eating.

Bolbitis heudelotii, found throughout tropical Africa in and alongside streams; a typical rheophyte with narrow leaflets. It can live totally submerged and has been introduced into Europe as an aquarium plant where its leaves help oxygenate the water.

The water horsetail (*Equisetum fluviatile*) spreading into a swampy pool in northern France. This species can form large stands in sour, peaty pools throughout the northern hemisphere.

The shore spleenwort, *Asplenium obtusatum*, has thick leathery leaves that are unaffected by salt water. It grows in similar coastal habitats in Australia, New Zealand (as here) and South America as *Asplenium marinum* in Western Europe.

much more finely cut than the sterile ones, and often produce axillary plantlets which quickly increase the size of the population. This plant is well-adapted to seasonal fluctuations in water level, as not only do the spores germinate under some depth of water, but the life-cycle from spore to spore can be completed in only 29 days! (A typical fern, such as the male fern, takes three years to do this.)

Closely related plants may live in very different habitats. Over 30 species of tropical ferns whose close relatives are part of the floor vegetation of rain forests are found growing in streams where the flow can change from a trickle to a torrent in a very short space of time. Plants adapted to this type of aquatic habitat are called *rheophytes* and have strong matted roots to hold them firmly, with tough fronds and narrow pinnae to give the least resistance to the strong water flow. Some of these rheophytes, for example *Microsorum pteropus*, may even shed their spores underwater.

A number of 'flowering' ferns, species of *Osmunda*, grow in wet swampy conditions and can brighten murky pools with their pale green fronds and tassels of golden-brown sporangia. Their ancient history is revealed in the chapter on The Fossil Record. In one species, *Osmunda claytoniana*, the fertile pinnae (leaf segments) are found in the middle portion of an otherwise sterile frond, giving it the name of interrupted fern. In other species, like the royal fern, *Osmunda regalis*, the fertile pinnae occur towards the apex of the frond like a spike of flowers, and are so reduced in width that they are barely distinguishable beneath the mass of sporangia. It grows throughout the world where there is unpolluted water to bathe its roots, ranging from acid bogs, stream and lakesides to maritime cliffs, and is a popular plant to grow beside garden ponds. Unlike most other ferns, species of *Osmunda* have sporangia that are rather simple in construction and gape open like a pair of clam-shells to release several hundred green spores.

Horsetails were amongst the most dominant plants of the world some 400 million years ago. Today they are found throughout all the major geographic areas except Australia and New Zealand, fringing lakes, both in the water and at the margins, and in swampy or very moist ground. The northern tundra and wet mountain flushes are also suitable habitats for horsetails, although here they are insignificant plants. In temperate zones, especially, there is a gradual change in the species making up the plant community as the land becomes dryer or richer in humus. Ancestral horsetails were amongst the pioneer plants of the first land masses. Their descendants reflect this in their ability to form colonies by means of their creeping underground stems and thus exploit suitable habitats to the maximum. Their leafless stems bear sporangia in whorled 'cones' as described in the Introduction.

The maritime habitat presents different problems to plants growing there, with the amount of salt being a major one. There are not many coastal ferns. The spleenworts (*Asplenium*) are a very large group of ferns that in the tropics grow as epiphytes on forest trees, but in temperate zones are mainly found on rocks and wooded banks. A few species grow only on seaside cliffs. The sea spleenwort, *Asplenium marinum*, of warm-temperate parts of Europe and north Africa, has rather fleshy, leathery fronds. It seems that it is not a need for salt that

The mangrove fern, *Acrostichum aureum*, seen here on the tidal mud flats in the island of Dominica. The fern makes large clumps reminiscent of the royal fern, but that species cannot withstand salt water.

confines it to such an inhospitable habitat, but rather its sensitivity to frost. The shore spleenwort, *Asplenium obtusatum*, is similar in appearance and habitat, but grows in the southern hemisphere from Chile across to Australia and New Zealand.

While the sea spleenwort does well to produce fronds 50 cm in length, the mangrove fern of the tropics, *Acrostichum aureum*, has stout fronds several metres tall that form an almost impenetrable fringe to these swamp areas. Its pinnae are very leathery and a welt of golden sporangia covers the lower surface of the fertile ones. Only a few other ferns are able to cope with a certain amount of salt in their habitat. Two of these, *Blechnum indicum* and *Cyclosorus interruptus*, might be termed weeds from their opportunist growth in the tropics and their ability to form extensive stands in coastal coconut plantations.

Previous page
Blechnum cycadifolium on the seaward slopes of
the south Pacific Robinson Crusoe Island (Juan
Fernández). The leaves of this fern resemble
those of a cycad and form a rosette on a short
trunk.

A wooded slope in the Olympic Mountains of
Washington State, USA, with a rich
assemblage of ferns, including the horseshoe
maidenhair fern (*Adiantum pedatum*) and
various shield ferns (*Polystichum* species).

Most of the world enjoys conditions where the constant humid heat of
the tropics and the fluctuations of temperature that make life so hard on
high mountains and in the polar regions are moderated and blended to
give a temperate climate. As the earth evolved to its present form, the
five major continents witnessed the full spectrum of climates.
Landmasses moved gradually as areas of the earth's crust expanded or
were subsumed. South America pulled away from one side of Africa, as
the Atlantic Ocean broadened, while on the other side India slid away
to create the Himalayas as it collided with Eurasia. Over the last one
million years, the ice-caps of the poles and mountain tops have
repeatedly advanced rapidly to cover vast areas and as quickly retreated.

Ferns of the temperate lands are a mixture of relics from warmer times
of 40–60 million years ago (the Lower Tertiary and Upper Cretaceous
periods) and their newly evolved descendants. The main groups are
relatively few compared to the numbers found in the richer tropics.
The species within these may show extremely complicated
interrelationships that have only recently been elucidated through
studies of their chromosomes and diagnostic chemicals. The
unravelling of the evolutionary history of two widespread temperate
genera, the spleenworts (*Asplenium*) and the buckler, male or wood
ferns (*Dryopteris*), reads like a detective story, with missing ancestors
and incestuous intermarriages that, coupled with bizarre reproductive
strategies, result in family trees as intricate as those of Europe's royalty.

The richest areas for ferns in the temperate zones are the moister ones
– the oceanic islands and land bordering the sea, or those mountain
valleys where cloud and mist prevail for at least part of the day. While
the Macaronesian islands of Madeira and the Azores have arisen as the
result of volcanic activity over the past 30 million years, the Canary
Islands were at least partly connected to the African continent. All
were colonized by fern spores borne on the winds from a moist and more
tropical Africa on the one hand, or from the equally subtropical areas of
Europe, on the other. The richest fern habitats are found at
600–1000 metres or more above sea-level, in the damper laurel and
heather forests that cling to the steep mountain sides of these high
volcanic islands. Thus the flora that once inhabited southern Europe
and Russia found a stronghold in the Canaries when the polar
glaciations of the late Tertiary period, a million or so years ago, drove
this vegetation type further south. Species such as *Diplazium caudatum*,
the primitive tree-fern, *Culcita macrocarpa*, and the chain fern,
Woodwardia radicans, survived in the gorges or *barrancos* of the
mountains when the forests were cleared on a large scale (mainly for
fuelwood to be used in sugarcane production) in the sixteenth and
seventeenth centuries. Populations of these are also found in the
remnants of ancient forests across the Iberian peninsula.

Outliers of the tropical filmy fern family, Hymenophyllaceae grow as
epiphytes on tree-heathers or on the walls of the steep, dark *barrancos*.
As the tundra of Europe receded towards the North Pole after the last
glaciations, the Tunbridge filmy fern (*Hymenophyllum tunbrigense*) and
the bristle fern (*Trichomanes speciosum*) spread northwards. On the
opposite side of the Atlantic Ocean, related species of filmy ferns
similarly recolonized the eastern states of the USA. In both North
America and Europe an interesting phenomenon has been discovered:

The primitive tree-fern, feto de cabalinho (*Culcita macrocarpa*), seen here in an old mineshaft in Portugal. This species is a relic of the once widespread Tertiary flora of Europe and is now found only in isolated sites in northern Iberia and in the Canary Islands, Azores and Madeira.

A ferny *barranco* in La Palma, Canary Isles, with species of *Athyrium, Diplazium, Dryopteris, Polypodium* and *Trichomanes speciosum*.

The kidney-leaved maidenhair fern (*Adiantum reniforme*), a common plant on more open rocks in the Canary Isles.

A rocky valley in Alabama, USA. The mossy growth on these sandstone rocks contains the dwarf bristle fern (*Trichomanes petersii*) whose prothallus or gametophyte has spread to the St Lawrence River some 750 miles beyond the range of the sporing plant.

the prothallus or gametophyte stage of the bristle fern, spreading by vegetative buds or gemmae to cover large areas of shady rock in northern regions way beyond the present range of the spore-bearing plant.

Prior to the last glaciation, the Mediterranean area was undergoing an extremely dry period when xerophytic ferns characteristic of arid zones (such as *Cheilanthes*, *Cosentinia* and *Notholaena*) would have grown from Spain across to the Caspian Sea. As the Alps were being formed in the early Tertiary Period, the sedimentary rocks laid down in earlier seas were pushed high. In some areas these uplifts were later eroded away, while others became isolated as damp islands in an inland sea. One such place was the Gorges du Verdon in south east France where there arose a species of spleenwort (*Asplenium jahandiezii*) which is found nowhere else. Why this species has not spread to other limestone areas in southern Europe is an enigma.

Elsewhere in northern and oceanic Europe ferns abound in the oak, birch and conifer forests. Carpets of the oak fern, *Gymnocarpium dryopteris*, the beech fern, *Phegopteris connectilis*, and many *Dryopteris* and *Polystichum* species dominate the floors of these woodland communities. Horsetails such as *Equisetum sylvaticum* grow with them in the wetter places. Similar assemblages of species are seen in the conifer belt of North America, while in the Rocky Mountain areas to the west, bathed by the Pacific mists, the northern maidenhair, *Adiantum pedatum*, can form an impressive sward. Many other species, for example, the hard or deer fern, *Blechnum spicant*, and the northern buckler or spreading wood fern, *Dryopteris expansa*, are found throughout the northern temperate zone.

The Verdon spleenwort (*Asplenium jahandiezii*), the rarest European fern and probably a relic from the fern flora that inhabited the Rhône valley area of France 25 million years ago.

Tip of the fertile leaf-lobe of the Killarney bristle fern (*Trichomanes speciosum*) showing the elongated 'bristle' bearing the closely packed sporangia. Note the green spores in the capsules, which, like those of the royal fern (*Osmunda*), must germinate immediately they are released or they will die.

The American climbing fern (*Lygodium palmatum*), a member of the more primitive family Schizaeaceae which is common in the tropics but grows as far north as southern New Hampshire.

The whisk fern (*Psilotum nudum*) on a warm, south-facing rock-face in southern Spain. This is a cosmopolitan species of the tropics that is also found in the warmer fringes of the temperate zones of both hemispheres.

The mother shield fern (*Polystichum proliferum*) growing in a gully and covered in hoare frost in Victoria, Australia.

A mid-montane temperate rain forest in the South Island of New Zealand, with a bank of hard ferns (*Blechnum* species) below the soft tree-fern (*Cyathea smithii*) showing the characteristic skirt of old leaf-stalks that shields the vulnerable growing point at the trunk apex from damage by invading epiphytes.

A similar climate to the Mediterranean is found in southern Africa, but here the fern flora was enriched by elements from tropical areas that pushed into South Africa from the north during a wetter Pleistocene period. Much of the vegetation is of the dry type described in the chapter on Arid Zones and is composed of *macchia* and other semi-desert communities, but there are also large areas of grassland (*veld*) with a varying degree of scrubland of various sorts in which ferns play only a minor role. Here are a number of Adiantaceae (*Cheilanthes*, *Pellaea*) and also the schizaeaceous genus *Mohria*. In the wetter riverine valleys where a forest community may develop, ferns like *Amauropelta bergiana* and *Dryopteris elongata* can be abundant.

The mountains of central Asia are for the most part too dry to be rich in ferns, but the deciduous and coniferous belt in the eastern Himalayas does have a wealth that excites the temperate fern gardener, with over 150 species of lady fern (*Athyrium*), bladder ferns (*Cystopteris*), wood or male ferns (*Dryopteris*) and shield ferns (*Polystichum*). The majority of these have still to be exploited for commercial cultivation, but their potential has been shown by a few introductions. In Japan there are over 80 species of *Dryopteris*, many of them in the colourful deciduous forests of beech, maple, chestnut and cherries. Here, too, grows *Adiantum pedatum*, many species of *Athyrium*, *Matteuccia*, with *Coniogramme intermedia*, *Dennstaedtia hirsuta*, *Osmunda japonica* and a host of others. There is an interesting similarity between the flora of Japan and eastern North America, with not only the example of *Adiantum* mentioned above, but with other species such as *Cryptogramma stelleri* and *Polypodium virginianum* common to both, reflecting their similar climates. The intermediate absences of these species are due again to the drastic effect of the Pleistocene glaciation that covered the whole of the boreal globe.

In the southern hemisphere the southern beech or *Nothofagus* forests of Victoria and Tasmania, and the *rata* (*Metrosideros*) woods of New Zealand have their own characteristic fern floras. *Blechnum* is common – not just one species as in the northern counterpart, but 12 or more. In mountainous districts with a high rainfall a temperate 'rain forest' develops where, like their tropical counterparts, tree ferns of the genera *Dicksonia* and *Cyathea* form a significant middle storey to the forest. When the larger shade-giving trees are felled the population of these species increases to such an extent that they are regarded by the forester as a secondary crop, providing strong fence posts for the farming community. Unlike their tropical cousins they are liable to be covered with snow, albeit for short periods. Genera that abound on the floors of these spectacular forests are, amongst others, *Adiantum*, *Asplenium*, *Doodia*, *Lastreopsis*, *Polystichum* and *Pteris*, whilst on trunks and rocks grow *Grammitis* and the filmy ferns, *Cardiomanes*, *Hymenophyllum* and *Trichomanes*.

Deciduous forest at 1600 metres in Nepal, with ▷ the trunks and branches of this mountain beech tree covered with the epiphyte *Polypodium lachnopus*.

Opposite page
A virgin hillside in Juan Fernández, showing a fine stand of the tree-fern *Thyrsopteris elegans*. This is very probably the most endangered fern species in the world, once found on the South American mainland, but now confined to this island.

A roadside verge beside a heathy bank in Gippsland, Victoria, Australia, with the swamp selaginella (*Selaginella uliginosa*) growing in wetter patches beneath the tangle fern (*Gleichenia dicarpa*).

In the comparable climatic zone in southern South America, Patagonian fitzroya and southern beech forests are the counterpart of those just described in Australasia, providing a habitat for the same or closely related species of ferns.

Open scrub areas and heathy margins in southern Australia have other interesting pteridophytes. In areas with little competition one can find the small *Phylloglossum drummondii*. This plant dies down each year and winters as an underground tuber. It has no close relatives and is found only in south east Australia and North Island of New Zealand. Lycopods such as *Lycopodium deuterodensum*, with the tangle fern, *Gleichenia microphylla*, may be dominant herbs of the roadside and damp, degraded pasture. In the proteaceous *Banksia* heathland is another unique species, *Selaginella uliginosa*, distantly related to *Selaginella selaginoides* of the northern bogs. Further north, in the subtropical grasslands of Queensland, many species of cloak ferns (*Cheilanthes*) and rock brakes (*Pellaea*) are found with the braid fern, *Platyzoma microphyllum*, a unique plant not found elsewhere.

The braid fern (*Platyzoma microphylla*) is a primitive fern of the dry, grassy scrub of Queensland, Australia. The felt of golden hairs on its rhizome enables it to survive occasional grass fires.

ARID ZONES

Previous page
Las Canadas, Tenerife.

Cheilanthes vellea in a lava field on Tenerife. The woolly felt on the leaves cuts down water loss through evaporation.

The sword fern, *Nephrolepis exaltata*, is an early colonizer of lava beds such as those in Lua Manu crater, Hawaii.

Life, as we know it, cannot exist without water, and the majority of plants require a constant supply to live, grow and reproduce successfully. There is, however, a wide range of habitats throughout the world where plants live without very much water. Of these, the tropical sandy deserts have the most extreme conditions and plants here must survive a virtual absence of rain. But there are other places where rainfall is either low or spasmodic, ranging from tropical and subtropical savannah, scrub and thornbush to rocky outcrops, screes, lava fields and even walls, to high mountains above the cloud level and to temperate sand dunes. In all these habitats there may be plants that condense their lives into the relatively short wet periods and survive drought conditions only as seeds. There are also, however, large numbers of species that are anatomically or physiologically modified to increase their uptake of water when it is available and to reduce the loss of it through evaporation. Such plants are called xerophytes.

As ferns and their allies might all be thought to need a constant supply of water, it is surprising how many of them live in arid zones. Many of these xerophytic pteridophytes are adapted in some way to survive periods of drought. Some live in very specific habitats, some have adapted their shape or appearance, others have modified their growth patterns or changed their reproductive cycles.

There are, for example, many parts of southern Africa and North America where the climate is very seasonal and the annual rainfall is concentrated into a few months of the year. Here the xerophytic ferns show a clear preference for living in rocky ground. In these areas there can be many small ferns rooted between rocks or in narrow cracks or fissures, finding there a measure of protection from the heat of the sun. This protection is all the better if the rocks are porous and retain rainwater for some time during the dry season.

Several species of the goldback and silverback ferns, such as *Pityrogramma calomelanos*, are opportunists because they rapidly colonize bare ground and are early invaders of man-made habitats such as roadside banks and cuttings. This particular fern is also one of the primary colonizers of volcanically devastated areas. This may seem unlikely, for the well-drained habitats of cooled lava fields appear completely inhospitable, offering neither soil nor water. These areas can, however, be colonized quickly by ferns, for the lava blocks are usually porous and act as reservoirs for any rain that may fall. The blocks are also pock-marked with surface vesicles, formed by escaping gas bubbles during the solidification of the lava, and the initial colonizers establish themselves in these vesicles. As the blocks degrade, other species of ferns, such as *Cheilanthes vellea* and *Nephrolepis exaltata*, will gradually invade the lava fields.

Many species of xerophytic ferns belong to the genera *Actiniopteris*, *Cheilanthes* and *Pellaea*. *Cheilanthes* is, perhaps, the most successful in having about two hundred species, including those sometimes referred to as *Notholaena*, and ranges in distribution from the tropics to many of the more temperate areas of the world.

Cheilanthes involuta growing in the moister places between boulders in woodland in the eastern Transvaal, South Africa.

Right above
Pellaea glabella has leathery leaves to withstand the dry conditions on dolomitic limestone cliffs at Niagara, Canada.

Notholaena sinuata, the wavy cloak fern, has densely scaly leaves adapted to such arid habitats as this in Baja California, Mexico, where it grows with cacti between boulders.

Actiniopteris pauciloba. A fire-resistant fern on a rocky outcrop in Zambia. New fronds are produced at the start of the rainy season.

The nodding clubmoss, *Lycopodium cernuum*, pictured here from near Buenaventura, Colombia, has shoots that arch over and root to form large colonies. The plants regenerate quickly from the rooted shoot-tips after fire has swept the area.

Lycopodium carolinianum in dambo grassland in Zambia during the rainy season. This clubmoss can produce tubers which survive fire to sprout when rain returns.

Opposite
Pellaea pectiniformis in the wet season, growing in Miombo woodland in Zambia. This fern produces buds which are protected by scaly old leaf bases against fires in the dry season.

Xerophytic ferns mostly have small, hairy or scaly fronds clustered tightly on short, stout rhizomes. The sori are protected by the reflexed margins of the frond segments. Many species that grow in the driest of habitats have dormant buds that are well protected against desiccation by being covered with old frond stalks and rhizome scales. In Zambia, for example, 95 out of the 146 species of pteridophytes growing in the dry savannah woodlands have such protected buds.

The growth pattern of xerophytic ferns depends directly on the weather. There is a burst of growth in the rainy seasons which ceases when dry conditions prevail. Some species are unable to survive dry spells unless their fronds die and the plant becomes dormant. Their rhizomes and hidden buds are either underground or at ground level where they are protected from the worst drying effects of the sun and the air. The dead fronds usually remain attached for several months although in some species they are shed as water becomes scarce. Other species curl up their fronds and often appear dead during prolonged droughts although they quickly revive again when moistened. Many of these ferns are also able to endure the fires that periodically sweep through open bush and savannah communities during the dry seasons, regenerating from their rhizomes when the rains return. Survival from burning is an extra advantage that has been conferred upon them and it is probable that fire has wiped out other, unadapted species that once grew in the area.

A number of clubmosses have wide ranges of moisture tolerance and some can also survive burning. The pantropical nodding clubmoss, *Lycopodium cernuum*, grows in a wide range of habitats from roadside verges to forest paths and from sea level to altitudes of 1500 metres. It spreads vegetatively by runner-like shoots, each of which divides to form an erect fertile axis before bending over to root. The colonies can be long-lived and regenerate from these rooted shoot-tips after fire has swept through them. Another widely distributed species, *Lycopodium carolinianum*, the slender clubmoss, produces small tubers on its creeping stems at the end of the wet season. These develop just below the level of the soil and so are unaffected by fire. When the wet season returns new shoots grow from these tubers to recolonize the area.

Actiniopteris radiata and *Selaginella imbricata* in dormant stages during the dry season in Zambia.

Selaginella imbricata in the wet season in Zambia. This clubmoss survives drought by closing the leaves round the stem.

The ability to survive severe water loss is not restricted to species growing in hot tropical and sub-tropical arid zones. Many others live in different but equally unfavourable conditions, such as *Jamesonia*, *Doryopteris* and *Anemia* in the high Andes above the tree-line. These are discussed in the chapter on Mountain Summits and Polar Regions. Then there are the temperate species that commonly grow on limestone rocks or in the mortar of old walls where rapid water run-off quickly leads to drought conditions. The European rusty-back fern, *Asplenium ceterach*, is an attractive example of ferns of these habitats. It is so well adapted to drought that it can survive the loss of 95 per cent of its water content. Although the plant then appears to be quite dead, it still fully recovers when moistened again.

Loss of water and the appearance of death is most pronounced in the so-called resurrection plants such as the African *Actiniopteris radiata*, *Cheilanthes inaequalis* and *Selaginella imbricata* and the American *Selaginella lepidophylla* and *Selaginella pilifera*. *Selaginella lepidophylla* became popular with collectors to sell as a novelty through its ability to curl when dry and unfurl when wet, even when dead. It has become rare in its native southern USA, Mexico and Central America.

Reproduction and dispersal are essential for the success of any plant if it is to spread into new habitats. Rhizome growth is very slow in xerophytic ferns so they tend to rely totally on spore production for dispersal. Certain species, including some of the goldback and silverback ferns, reach maturity remarkably quickly thus allowing the species to spread rapidly within the new habitat.

Although they may have a speedy life cycle, many arid zone species are further adapted to counteract any environmental stress encountered at the different stages. Spores must not germinate too easily in case there is insufficient water for the complete growth of the small prothallus or gametophyte that bears the sex organs, and thus many spores have elaborately ornamented walls to prevent small quantities of water triggering a growth response. Even if there is sufficient water to ensure the full growth of the prothallus there may not be enough for fertilization, as there has to be free surface water on the prothallus to enable the male sperm to swim to a female egg-containing archegonium. However, many arid zone ferns do not rely on sexual fertilization. Instead, they form new plants directly from prothallial tissue as part of the process known as apogamy. The new sporelings will grow and become independent much faster than sexually formed ones thereby lessening the time when they are most susceptible to drought.

A high proportion of xerophytic ferns have very restricted distributions and are said to be endemics. In southern Africa, for example, there are many species of *Cheilanthes* and *Pityrogramma* that grow nowhere else, and for this reason the region is thought to have been a centre for cheilanthoid fern speciation, spurred on by the violent climatic fluctuations that took place during the last one to two million years.

Asplenium ceterach growing on a wall in Germany. This fern revives even after losing 95 per cent of its water content.

Cheilanthes inaequalis. A resurrection fern growing on a rocky outcrop in Zambia. The younger fronds are active while the older ones are still dormant.

Isoetes velata on Roque Haute, southern France in a drying pool during the summer. This quillwort has an underground corm that survives the drought.

There is another group of tropical pteridophytes that grow in seasonal pools and wet marshes. One is a fern, *Marsilea*, looking very much like four-leaved clover, and the other is the quillwort, *Isoetes*, which is also found at the bottom of deep mountain lakes. Both produce two kinds of spores, microspores and megaspores, which eventually provide the sperm and egg respectively. When the water shrinks and evaporates during the dry season their perennating organs are either buried underground or lie on the drying mud whence they can be dispersed by wind or animals to new areas.

Marsilea has its sporangia in thick-walled bean-like structures, called sporocarps, attached at the base of leaves to the horizontal rhizome. They can be produced in such abundance that the Australian aboriginal people have ground them for flour to make bread. These sporocarps are very resistant to desiccation but open on the return of water to release the spores and permit sexual reproduction and the formation of new sporelings.

Isoetes has its sporangia sunk into the bases of its quill-like leaves which are attached to a small, swollen corm-like stem. This underground corm enables those plants growing in ephemeral pools to survive periods of drought. The return of water can prompt the release of the spores although there is evidence that worms and snails may aid in spore dispersal.

Drynaria rigidula growing on an exposed rock face in SE Asia. This fern has broad leaf bases which collect humus that holds water to tide the plant through dry periods.

The clover-fern, *Marsilea quadrifolia*, growing at the edge of a rice field in northern ▷ Italy. Hard, bean-like reproductive structures called sporocarps are produced that are very drought-resistant, but which germinate quickly in wet conditions.

Previous page
Mount Osorno, rising to 2600 m in Chile.

Huperzia trancilla, in the *paramo* of Ecuador.
The white-tipped leaves of this clubmoss deflect
the strong sunlight.

Mountains – bleak, imposing, mysterious, homes of gods in many mythologies and also home to a variety of lycopsids and ferns, despite their inhospitable terrain and environment.

The high Andes of South America show some of the most curious examples of adaptation to the difficult conditions found above the tree-line. This wet and windy habitat, at an altitude of 3000–4000 m, is called *paramo*. The temperature ranges from 20°c during the day to −2°c at night. Here, sheltered amongst tussocks of grasses and mosses between shrubs and giant herbs, grow brush-like clumps of clubmosses, species of *Lycopodium* and other genera, in assorted colours: shades of red, yellow-green or frosted with white leaf-tips. The additional pigments screen the plants from the high levels of ultra-violet light found at this altitude. Some species have creeping subterranean stems which, protected by other plants from the extremes of weather, enable one individual to form a colony often several metres across. The aerial shoots borne by these stems become independent plants if the creeping stem dies. Other clubmosses grow in neat clusters of compact branches up to 50 cm tall. The leaves of all species are covered by a thick, waxy cuticle which both prevents dehydration during the hot days and gives some insulation at night.

Clubmosses are pioneer plants and are, as such, to be found in the highest vegetation zones of mountains round the globe. Some species have a very wide distribution, occurring throughout the World. Others have a disjunct pattern of distribution reflecting the evolution of the earth's landmasses and their climatic history.

Huperzia kuesteri, shrouded in mist in the
paramo of Ecuador.

Huperzia crassa, in the *paramo* of Ecuador. The red pigment in the leaves helps to protect this clubmoss against high levels of ultra-violet light.

Paramo at 4000 m in Colombia.

Jamesonia canescens, in the *paramo* of Venezuela. This fern has a dense mat of hairs to protect it against the harsh conditions.

Papuapteris linearis, New Guinea. This close relative of the ubiquitous shield-ferns is endemic to the alpine grassland of New Guinea.

Isoetes andina, Costa Rica. Quillworts like this one are often the dominant plant of high altitude mountain lakes.

The fern *Jamesonia*, similar to these clubmosses in size and with erect fronds rising from a creeping rhizome, grows with them in the *paramo*. Its small, tough leaflets are almost clenched together, and in some species the developing sporangia are protected by a mat of tangled hairs. This habit is shared by an unrelated Australasian fern, *Papuapteris*, from the alpine grassland of Papua New Guinea. *Papuapteris* is of similar size, but produces its fronds in clusters from a vertical stem.

At slightly lower altitudes, but still above the tree-line, ferns may have to endure not only frost but also fire. Although fire is traditionally used by man in many parts of the world as an aid to clearing land for agriculture or to drive out game animals, there are areas, for example, in southern Africa and Australasia where fires have been a natural and regular phenomenon for aeons. The native plants are therefore capable of surviving fire, and may indeed require scorching to complete their life cycles. In southern Africa one of the tree-ferns, *Cyathea dregei*, is able to grow at an astonishing range of altitudes, spanning sea-level to nearly 2000 m. Always a lover of full sun, it develops a stem up to 5 m tall and 45 cm in diameter that is surmounted by a whorl of fronds some 2–3 m long. This stout trunk enables it to survive most fires unscathed, whilst the densely scaled croziers unfurl anew after fire or frost has killed the expanded fronds.

High altitude mountain lakes round the world are cold (2°–4°c) and crystal clear. They are frequently low in nutrients and therefore support few plants. A dominant, if not the sole plant inhabitant of some of these lakes, is the quillwort. These aquatic lycopsids grow at the bottom of the lakes as spiky rosettes of narrow, usually cylindrical leaves and are totally immersed except during periods of exceptional drought. This primitive plant has spores of two kinds: large megaspores and miniscule microspores. A sporangium contains one size or the other, and although, as in the clubmosses, each leaf bears only one sporangium, in quillworts this structure is half-sunken in the leaf tissue. There is no active mechanism to release the spores. The leaves decay to expose the sporangia which may disperse a short distance before they too disintegrate to liberate either numerous megaspores or a multitude of microspores.

Cyathea dregei, in the alpine grassland of the Republic▷ of South Africa. This tree-fern endures frost and fire.

Dipteris conjugata, Borneo. This fern with fan-shaped fronds is found growing on the well-drained slopes of mountain ridges and landslips in SE Asia. The reddish colour of the young fronds protects them against the strong sunlight.

On well-drained slopes of ridges and landslips, in the summit zones of the mountains of South East Asia, species of *Dipteris* grow at around 1500 m. The young, expanding fronds are reddish in colour and this extra pigmentation protects the tissue from the strong sunlight. Their oddly-shaped fronds are up to 50 cm long and have sporangia scattered along the veins of their lower surface. These ridges also support the striking fern *Matonia*, with its curiously branched, fan-like fronds that may attain a length of 1 m.

Small thickets of some species of *Gleichenia* are found on the ridges of mountains throughout Asia, Australasia and the tropics of Central and South America. Extreme exposure may cause these ferns to arrest their frond development at an early stage, so that the plants produce only 50 cm long, unbranched or once-branched fronds. In some species, the lamina segments are almost cupped round the sori, and a dense felt of scales and hairs may give further protection to the sorus (group of sporangia).

The alpine belt is found at varying altitudes on different mountains around the world according to their latitude and isolation from one another. For example, at similar latitudes the alpine belt is lower on the mountains of South East Asia than on the mountains in South America because the former are not part of a massive chain like the Andes. The alpine belt is also found at lower altitudes with an increase in latitude. Hence, in the Arctic and Antarctic zones, the alpine belt and the tundra are one and the same.

As well as altitude, the distribution of rainfall is also important in causing the development of the alpine belt. In wetter places, such as Mount Kinabalu close to the equator in Sabah, Borneo, and mountains of Eurasia, North America and New Zealand, the forest belt is succeeded by the alpine belt. But on dryer mountains the alpine belt may be above a semi-desert belt, as in most of the South American Andes. Other mountains, such as Pico de Teide on Tenerife, one of the Canary Islands, rise above the clouds and there is no alpine belt as the forest gives way to desert-like vegetation at the summit. Plants living at a high altitude near the season-less equator may endure a diurnal variation in temperature that plants growing at higher latitudes, with very little diurnal variation, experience from one season to another.

Whilst some ferns and lycopsids are found only on mountains, others use their pioneering qualities to grow also on the vast expanses of the northern tundra. Here the land has only relatively recently been released from the grip of glacier blankets and, as on mountains heights, has soil that is low in nutrients amongst areas of bare rock. Pteridophytes are great opportunists. Their spores can survive, travelling in air currents for possibly thousands of kilometres, to germinate in cracks and crevices of weathered rock. Ferns have thin, wiry roots which are able to exploit the minute cracks in weathered rocks, anchoring the plant and securing moisture.

Various species of *Woodsia* are found around the world on mountains and also in the northern tundra. These ferns are rather delicate in appearance and may be only a few centimetres long, but the dense mat of scales on the fronds partially shields them from the effects of wind and

Matonia foxworthyi, Borneo.
This fern is found only on the mountain ridges of SE Asia.

Woodsia alpina, Scotland.
A fern of the alpine belt and the northern tundra.

Gleichenia alpina, Tasmania. A sun-loving fern that survives the extreme conditions on high mountains by arresting its frond development at an early stage. It produces taller and more branched fronds in sheltered places at lower altitudes.

Cryptogramma crispa, Germany. Parsley-fern has dimorphic fronds. The narrower, more finely cut ones bear the sori.

Polystichum lonchitis, Scotland. A tough-leaved fern growing in the shelter of crevices and boulders in the high mountains.

Cryptogramma crispa & Athyrium distentifolium, Norway. These ferns are two that seek the shelter of boulders to grow in arctic alpine habitats.

cold. Their taller companion ferns, both in the tundra and on North American and Eurasian mountains, include species of *Polystichum*, *Athyrium* and *Dryopteris*. These mountain relatives of woodland species, often grow in very sheltered places that have a microclimate similar to that of a wood. The crowns of these may be so well sheltered, deep at the base of boulder scree, that only the tips of their fronds protrude into the open. *Athyrium distentifolium* grows where it is covered deeply enough by the winter snow to be insulated from the severe cold.

Species of *Cryptogramma* may also be found where snow lies deeply. These ferns have dimorphic fronds: the vegetative ones have broad segments, whilst the fertile fronds have the margins of the segments curled back over the sori to give a much more finely cut appearance and are held more erect. *Cryptogramma crispa* grows on rock ledges or at the more stable margins of scree slopes.

With the onset of winter the fronds of ferns in these habitats die, save for *Woodsia*, whose dead fronds are shed like the leaves of a deciduous tree. In other non-evergreen ferns, the fronds merely drop down to deflect the worst weather away from the crowns during the course of the season and gradually decay months later.

Most unfern-like are the moonworts. These fleshy plants, often only a few centimetres tall, are true ferns, despite their lack of the classic coiled crozier and are found in the coldest temperate regions around both Poles. Their roots exchange nutrients with a fungus (a mycorrhizal association), to the benefit of both organisms. In their earliest stages, each frond is encased in a curious sheath which ruptures as the frond expands. Each frond has two distinct parts: a vegetative blade with fan-like segments and a finely-branched fertile spike that bears the sporangia. Even these spore-producing structures differ from the typical fern form in that they do not have the elaborate mechanism for flinging out a relatively small number of spores. Instead, the thick-walled sporangia gape open, releasing many thousands of spores to be blown away by the wind.

Botrychium lunaria, Germany. Moonworts are most unfern-like ferns with their fleshy fronds being partly a branched spike laden with sporangia.

The alpine belt habitat of *Athyrium distentifolium* & *Cryptogramma crispa* in Norway.

Previous page
Flooded rice fields in Indonesia.

The spores of the male fern, *Dryopteris filix-mas*, were once thought to cause the wearer to be invisible. The stem yields both a vermifuge and a perfumed oil.

Below left to right
The attractive ostrich fern, *Matteuccia struthiopteris*, whose croziers are widely eaten in North America.
Croziers of the ostrich fern on sale in the United States of America.
The crozier of the ostrich fern, *Matteuccia struthiopteris*, eaten as a vegetable.

Since prehistory, plants have helped man in many ways, providing food, clothing, utensils, shelter, medicine and a pleasing environment. Ferns and the allied lycopsids continue to contribute to our well-being, and although they are no longer credited by western society with magical powers, people from countries where traditional medicine is practised still believe in their mystical properties.

A common fern in North America and across Europe and Asia is the male fern, *Dryopteris filix-mas*, which has been used for at least eighteen centuries to rid people of intestinal worms. Despite being such a powerful vermifuge, the stem was also used in love philtres in medieval times, and the fern was thought to have mystical powers as well. The young croziers, once called St John's Hands, were believed to give protection against sorcery and the evil eye, while the 'seeds' conferred the power of invisibility. An oil from the stem gave rise to the Fougère genre of perfumes, although these are now made synthetically.

Bracken is perhaps the most ubiquitous fern in the world. It was credited from at least the twelfth century with magical powers, because the cross-section of its stem and leaf-stalk revealed a complex pattern of tissues that could be taken as the sign of Christ. The practical uses to which bracken has been put are immensely varied. The large fronds have been used for thatching buildings, providing bedding for farm animals and for packing market produce across the world from Europe to South East Asia. Young, furled fronds have been widely eaten in Japan, the Philippines, Africa, Europe and the USA [NB The reader is most strongly advised not to sample them as this fern is now known to contain carcinogenic chemicals.] Similarly, croziers of the non-toxic ostrich fern, *Matteuccia struthiopteris*, are sold in North America, especially in Canada, fresh, frozen or canned, while in South East Asia those of another fern, *Diplazium esculentum*, are widely eaten. Tests on the ostrich fern have not found any known carcinogens. The stem of bracken contains starch which has been eaten in the Canary Islands and Australasia, and even used for brewing beer in Scandinavia.

Young bracken fronds, *Pteridium aquilinum*, unfurling in Ghana. Although it is now regarded as a troublesome weed in many places, this fern used not only to be credited with magical powers but had a wide range of uses, from thatching to glass-making.

Bracken showing its autumn colours in a woodland clearing in England.

Both the stem and fronds of bracken have been used to dye wool and silk in the northern hemisphere. Different mordants give a range of colours from deep yellow through a series of greens to black. The fronds are a source of strong fibres that may be used as twine, and have even been used as fiddle strings in Borneo. Ashes from burnt fronds provide an alkali once used for making soap in Japan and glass in Europe.

The evergreen horsetail, *Equisetum hyemale*, with its stem rough with silica granules, was used in Europe from medieval to relatively recent times as a pot scourer and as a fine abrasive for polishing wood. At the same time, on the opposite side of the world, the Chinese knew this plant as a useful medicine for diseases of both the liver and the eye. Its usefulness in treating liver complaints was also known in Europe, and it is still harvested in Norway and the silica extracted for this purpose. Recent clinical trials in China have shown its effectiveness in the treatment of acute infectious hepatitis. Bundles of stems were used as mantles in the early days of gas lighting. A very common species of horsetail, *Equisetum arvense*, was eaten like asparagus shoots by the Romans and North American Indians and has also been used to treat sore mouths in the West Indies and painful joints in Malaysia. It is exported to many countries from France for preparing clarinet reeds. Other uses of horsetails include promoting fertility in women, treating acne and ulcers and as an ingredient of modern cosmetic lotions.

Majestic tree-ferns of the tropics and sub-tropics have stems strong enough to be used as posts in the construction of huts. This strength, combined with the patterns of different tissues in the stem, allows the creation of beautiful vases. Sadly, these lovely ferns are being sacrificed to the demands of some horticulturalists. They are felled to strip off the fibrous mass of roots encasing their stems which has found great favour recently as a growing medium for orchids.

The stems of the horsetail, *Equisetum hyemale*, are rough with silica granules that are valuable for treating liver complaints and make this plant useful as an abrasive.

Equisetum arvense, a common horsetail, which has been eaten like asparagus as well as used medicinally.

A vase carved from the trunk of a tree-fern in Réunion. The different internal tissues of the stem form the pattern.

Tall tree-ferns on an Indonesian hillside. ▷

Tree-fern stems being used as the uprights in the construction of a building in Papua New Guinea.

Asplenium trichomanes, the maidenhair spleenwort, used as a laxative and to treat chest infections as well as to ward off evil.

Man-made clearings, trail and roadsides at low altitudes in the tropics are rapidly colonized by the sun (or scrambling) fern, *Dicranopteris*, a fern that is capable of indefinite growth. The strands of vascular tissue within the frond midribs are very supple and can be woven into such diverse goods as hats and cigar cases. The whole midribs are very strong and, tied in bundles, they can be used for making marine fish traps. Single midribs may be split to be used as pens.

Rice is widely grown in the tropics of the Old World to provide the staple carbohydrate food of a large percentage of the world's population. Long term crop monoculture requires the use of fertilizer to prevent the soil becoming depleted of certain nutrients with a resulting decline in harvest. In the early stage of rice cultivation the fields are flooded with water, and this enables a curious fern, which provides a natural fertilizer, to be grown. The tiny *Azolla* plants, only 1–2 cm long, are free-floating. Their leaves are only about 1 mm long, but have two lobes, the lower of which houses a nitrogen-fixing alga. This green manure may be left to rot as the field dries out to provide a top dressing, or may be harvested separately to be ploughed into the soil before the rice is planted. The green floating sward of *Azolla*, sometimes called the mosquito fern, is also found in temperate zones on the still waters of ponds and lakes, or on slow-flowing rivers and canals.

The medicinal uses of ferns cover a wide spectrum. Fevers, worm infections, chest complaints and blood disorders are treated by a variety of ferns worldwide. The early herbalists used the *Doctrine of Signatures* to determine how plants were to be used medicinally. This philosophy held that nature had given a plant a particular shape to its leaves and flowers to help man know which ailment the plant would cure. The true spleenwort of Dioscorides, who wrote the earliest known herbal called *De materia medica* in the first century AD, is *Asplenium ceterach*, illustrated and discussed in the chapter on Arid Zones. It was thought to resemble the spleen and hence both the common name spleenwort and the Latin name of *Asplenium* are used for this group of ferns which were credited with the power to cure enlarged spleens, and also liver and kidney complaints. It was recommended that the leaves should be boiled in wine and the liquor drunk within forty days to cure infirmities of the spleen. Species of this genus were also used as medicine for other ailments. *Asplenium trichomanes*, for example, is found in Australia, the Americas and Eurasia and has been used to treat chest infections, and as a laxative in India and Europe. In parts of Europe this fern was also credited with averting such evils as witchcraft.

Above right
The scrambling fern, *Dicranopteris linearis*, colonizing a bank at the edge of the forest in Malaysia. The frond midribs are strong enough to use to make pens and fishtraps.

The mosquito fern, *Azolla*, lives on the surface of water. It is used as a fertilizer for ▷ rice fields because it harbours blue-green algae which fix gaseous nitrogen from the atmosphere into organic molecules.

The maidenhair fern, *Adiantum capillus-veneris*, is native to most countries of the world and has been used in the cure of a vast range of ailments from insanity to rickets.

Tubs made from tree-fern stems on sale in Réunion.

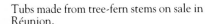

The dainty maidenhair fern, *Adiantum capillus-veneris*, grows naturally in the tropical and warmer temperate regions of both the northern and southern hemispheres, and is a popular house plant in cooler countries. It almost merits status as the panacea fern, being credited round the world as a curative for asthma, snake bites, diseases of the spleen, breast, liver and kidneys, 'stones', rickets, insanity, smallpox and centipede bites. It is also used as a cough syrup and to promote growth of head and beard hair. Its relatives have some of the same powers, but have also been used in North America and Japan to stop bleeding and to treat leprosy in West Africa.

Through the centuries, the theory behind the use of plants for medicine has changed greatly. Homeopathy, a field of 'alternative medicine', was developed about a century ago. The stag's horn clubmoss, *Lycopodium clavatum*, which is found in most arctic-alpine habitats of the world, and has a long history of magical and medicinal uses, is now used in this way. The entire plant was dried and used in medieval times in Europe to cure eczema and scurvy, to heal wounds, and for use as a diuretic in the treatment of dropsy, gout and kidney ailments. The spores are very smooth and repel water and were used as baby powder in the seventeenth century. More recently, in the guise of 'vegetable sulphur', they have been used to coat pills. The high oil content of the spores made them a useful ingredient of fireworks and early flashlights for photography. In southern Africa this plant has been used as a diuretic and antispasmodic as well as being smoked to relieve headaches. The development of homeopathic treatment has widened its field of use to encompass relief of symptoms as varied as hiccups, premenstrual tension, period pains, cystitis, irritability, dislike of exercise and fear of failure, whilst reinstating its validity in the treatment of gout.

There is a current upsurge in ethnobotanical surveys linked with chemical analysis to discover the active ingredients of plants long used by people all round the world. These may reveal a wider range of modern medicinal uses for ferns and related plants.

Spores of the stag's horn clubmoss, *Lycopodium clavatum*, are used to coat pills and ▷ have been an ingredient for fireworks. This plant is used in homeopathic medicine to treat a variety of complaints which include premenstrual tension and gout.

Previous page
The magnificent Victorian fernery at Kibble Palace, Glasgow, Scotland.

An attractive collage of ferns from a Jamaican fern album.

Ferns do not have a long history of popularity as cultivated plants. House plants had been popular for many years in countries with a long, dark winter season, but it was not until the middle of the nineteenth century that new techniques were developed for cultivating ferns in climates and localities highly alien to their natural preferences. At this time there was also such a widespread social preoccupation with death in northern countries and their colonies, that the advent of ferns with their evergreen foliage was greeted with great enthusiasm. Today, towards the end of the twentieth century, ferns are increasingly popular to brighten the rather cramped modern homes and gardens of many countries.

The gloomy living conditions and industrial pollution prevalent in many cities of the colder countries in the mid-eighteen hundreds were death to all but the toughest house plants. Whilst the main nurseries and botanical gardens were able to raise exotic ferns from spores collected abroad, it was the discovery (credited to Nathaniel Ward of London) that closed glass cases protected plants from even such rigours as transatlantic sea voyages, that enabled more house plants to be easily grown. This led to the fashion for growing ferns in often highly elaborate 'Wardian cases', as they were called, in the living rooms of the more well-to-do. These provided a sealed environment that kept the humidity, temperature and air quality stable enough for even the most delicate ferns to grow. On a larger scale, decorative greenhouses were built in botanic gardens or added onto houses as conservatories. If heated, these were suitable for growing such plants as tropical orchids and exotic fruits. However, ferns always had the advantage of being attractive throughout the seasons with evergreen growth in a great diversity of form. They were an important feature of 'winter gardens', the name often given to such greenhouses. It was fashionable for ladies to compile picturesque albums of pressed plants or to make items of fancy work such as blotters decorated with the outline of a dainty fern frond produced by splattering ink.

The first books devoted entirely to the culture of ferns were produced in Europe in the latter half of the nineteenth century. Some were merely expanded nursery catalogues, others explained the principles of taxonomic classification into genera, families and orders, and how to grow ferns from spores, with descriptions of the different species, noting their native country and their horticultural requirements with methods of pest control. The native, non-exotic ferns were not neglected either as they could be grown as border plants or in 'ferneries', rockeries built in the semblance of natural grottoes. In Britain, the rarity of some species and the wealth of naturally produced sports or varieties, however monstrous, were grossly exploited for an eager market of both indoor and outdoor growers. While several of the rarer species were almost exterminated, the lists of varieties of just a few species reached about a thousand.

A Wardian case, from the Peoples' Palace ▷
Museum, Glasgow, Scotland.

The cover of an album of New Zealand ferns at the Natural History Museum, London, England, made of inlaid wood from native trees.

Two cultivated varieties, 'ramosum Feizor' and 'crispum' of the hart's tongue fern, *Asplenium scolopendrium*.

The maidenhair spleenwort, *Asplenium trichomanes*, takes on a fancy form as the cultivated variety 'ramo-cristata'.

In the constantly hot tropics where the daylength does not vary through the year, the custom of growing plants inside houses did not develop. Here, where homes are relatively sparsely furnished to allow for as much air circulation as possible, and where the luxuriant vegetation harbours more animal pests and moulds than those of temperate regions, house plants would be detrimental, rather than beneficial, to man and his buildings. However, steps and verandas, and the trunks of nearby trees are good niches for growing a selection of jungle flowers and ferns that appeal to man's artistic nature.

Each fertile fern frond typically produces millions of spores, of which perhaps only one or two succeed in producing a new generation. The typical life cycle of a fern is explained simply in the Introduction. If living plants are taken from their wild habitats, species may quickly become extinct. International laws prevent export of certain species from their native lands and many countries have national laws to protect plants. Only rarely is it morally or criminally wrong to remove a pinna (leaf segment) to collect the spores to grow an attractive fern oneself. Whilst spores germinate readily on moist soil or rocks in a humid atmosphere, the resulting prothalli or gametophytes are easily killed off by competition from mosses, moulds and algae that also thrive in the same environment. The early gardeners often used pieces of naturally porous rock such as tufa or fragments of terracotta pots to germinate spores on, and they scrubbed them as clean as possible to get the prothalli off to a good start. Sousing soil with boiling water is also fairly effective. Pressure cookers and, more recently, microwave ovens have made it easy to sterilize soil and flowerpots. Once the soil and pots are cool, but still damp, the dust-like spores are lightly sprinkled on. A sheet of glass over the top keeps the humidity high and prevents contamination from air-borne moss, fungal and algal spores. After a few weeks in a shady place the soil usually becomes covered in a green sward as the spores germinate and the prothalli develop. It is important that these little plants are not too closely packed (if they are, they should be carefully pricked out without allowing them to dry out) and are kept damp so that there is a thin film of water over them to enable sexual reproduction to take place. Before long, small leaves appear that are often very different to the frond from which the spores were collected. The sporeling plants should be pricked off as soon as they are big enough to handle, but must be kept covered to ensure high humidity. As they grow, the covering is gradually kept less close, allowing the humidity of the air surrounding the plants to decrease gradually until they are well hardened off. No gardener can fail to be excited by producing new ferns from invisible spores, and this emotion is matched by the amazement of the most unskilled plantsman when an unexpected fern appears, apparently from nowhere, in the pot of another plant. Spores of many species are available from some of the fern societies listed in the Appendix.

But where is the new fern to grow? The previous chapters have illustrated the great diversity of natural habitats of ferns. Some grow in the wettest places, some on the branches of the tallest trees and others in the crevices of apparently dry rock; some evolved in tropical countries, others in a frosty temperate climate. Plants live best in conditions as close as possible to those of their natural environment,

An attractive cultivar, 'divisilobum', of the soft shield fern, *Polystichum setiferum*.

The slender shoots of an evergreen horsetail, *Equisetum hyemale*, beside a pool, contrast with the round leaves of the king-cup.

One of the Boston ferns, *Nephrolepis pendula*, from Central and South America makes a handsome house plant.

but many can cope with less than ideal conditions. This is the reason so many house plants in temperate countries are known as 'foliage plants', because they struggle slowly on in artificial habitats that do not give them the impetus to produce flowers.

Tender ferns, those from tropical or subtropical countries, may be grown with care as house plants. Most dislike the full force of sunlight, and the dry atmosphere of a centrally heated home is best relieved by regularly spraying the fern with water. Very popular examples are the bird's nest fern (*Asplenium nidus*), maidenhair fern (*Adiantum capillus-veneris*) and Boston fern (*Nephrolepis exaltata*); the magnificent stag's horn ferns (*Platycerium* species) require more nurturing. Such ferns will grow happily outside in the warmer, frost-free temperate regions such as the southern areas of the USA and China and the northern parts of New Zealand. Lath houses make attractive garden features, giving both ferns and gardeners welcome shade.

Lycopodium carinatum, an attractive clubmoss.

Asplenium nidus, the bird's nest fern, is a popular house plant.

The blue appearance of this clubmoss, *Selaginella uncinata*, is not due to a pigment, but results from the way light is diffracted by the surface of the leaves.

Variegation is rare amongst the ferns and related plants, but is displayed here in a clubmoss, *Selaginella martensii*.

Majestic tree-ferns, *Dicksonia antarctica*, tower above a bed of *Blechnum tabulare*.

The same attention paid to furnishing a room with a pleasing scheme of colours and shapes in the form of furnishings, paintings and plants is necessary to make a garden attractive. Successful landscaping composes a variety of forms and colour, whether plants, land formations or buildings, into a mutually enhancing arrangement and different parts of a garden are keynotes as the seasons change. Ferns can take an important role, providing a wide range of size, texture and shades of green that can either complement each other in the shady parts, or set off the colours and forms of flowering plants through the year. Shaggy croziers unfurling in the spring above a carpet of flowering bulbs gives movement to the scene. The water-loving royal ferns, *Osmunda* species, form striking clumps that tower over most other water-side plants. The alpine enthusiast fares well, with both leathery and feathery ferns whose fronds press against rock faces or emerge in clusters from crevices.

Although it may be that the '*Earth laughs in flowers*' (R. W. Emerson), remember also Thoreau's words, '*Nature made ferns for pure leaves, to see what she could do in that line*'.

Blechnum marinum with its slender, erect fertile fronds gives form to a raised bed of mixed ferns as it grows here in front of a lady fern (*Athyrium filix-femina*).

A beautifully landscaped garden with a clump of ▷ the royal fern, *Osmunda regalis*, in the foreground.

Snow dusting a group of varieties of *Polystichum setiferum*, the soft shield fern.

The bright cultivar 'foliosum Moly's Green' of the soft shield fern, *Polystichum setiferum*.

SELECTED BOOKS FOR FURTHER READING

Abbe, E. 1981. *The Fern Herbal.* Cornell University Press, New York. ISBN 0–8014–1718-x

Brownsey, P. J. & Smith-Dodsworth, J. C. 1989. *New Zealand ferns and allied plants.* David Bateman Ltd, Aukland. ISBN 1–86953-003–9

Burrows, J. E. 1990. *Southern African ferns and fern allies.* Sandton, Fransden Publishers. ISBN 0–620-14616–8

Cody, W. J. & Britton, D. M. 1989. *Ferns and fern allies of Canada.* Canadian Government Publishing Centre, Ottawa. ISBN 0–660-13102–1

Dyer, A. F. & Page, C. N. (Eds). 1985. Biology of Pteridophytes. *Proceedings of the Royal Society of Edinburgh* **86**B. ISSN 0308–2113

Goudey, C. J. 1988. *A handbook of ferns for Australia and New Zealand.* Lothian Publishing Company Pty Ltd, Port Melbourne. ISBN 0–85091-282–2

Grounds, R. 1974. *Ferns.* Pelham Books Ltd., London. ISBN 0–7207-0687–4

Hoshizaki, B. J. 1976. *Fern growers manual.* Alfred A. Knopf, New York. ISBN 0–394-49687–6

Jones, D. L. 1987. *Encyclopaedia of Ferns.* British Museum (Natural History), London. ISBN 0–565-01019–0

Jones, D. L. & Clemesha, S. C. 1981 (2nd ed.). *Australian ferns and fern allies.* Reed Books Pty, Frenchs Forest. ISBN 0–589-50265–4

Kaye, R. 1968. *Hardy ferns.* Faber & Faber, London. SBN 571082084 [out of print]

Kurata, S. & Nakaike, T. (Eds). 1979–1987. *Illustrations of pteridophytes of Japan* (5 vols). University of Tokyo Press, Tokyo.
vol 1 has no ISBN
vol 2 ISBN 0–86008-381–0
vol 3 ISBN 0–86008-333–0
vol 4 ISBN 4–13-061064–3, 0–86008-381–0
vol 5 ISBN 4–13-061065–1, 0–86008-407–8

Lellinger, D. B. 1985. *A field manual of the ferns and fern allies of the United States and Canada.* Smithsonian Institute, Washington. ISBN 0–87474-602–7, 0–87474-603–5

May, L. W. 1978. The economic uses and associated folklore of ferns and fern allies. *The Botanical Review* **44**: 491–528. ISSN 0006–8101

Mickel, J. 1979. *The home gardener's book of ferns.* Holt, Rinehart & Winston, New York. ISBN 0–03–045736-x, 0–03-045741–6

Murillo, M. T. 1983. *Usos de los helechos en Suramrica con especial referencia a Colombia.* Universidad Nacional de Colombia, Bogota. no ISBN

Page, C. N. 1988. *The New Naturalist Ferns, their habitats in the British and Irish Landscape.* Collins, London. ISBN 0–00-219383–3, 0–00-219382–5

Piggott, A. G. 1988. *Ferns of Malaysia in colour.* Tropical Press SDN BHD., Kuala Lumpur. ISBN 967–73-0029–6

Prelli, R. 1990 (2nd ed.). *Guide des fougères et plantes alliés.* Éditions Lechavalier, Paris. ISBN 2–720-50528–5

Sporne, K. R. 1975 (4th ed.). *The morphology of pteridophytes.* Hutchinson & Co. (Publishers) Ltd, London. ISBN 0–09-123860–9, 0–09-123861–7 [out of print]

Thomas, B. A. 1981. *The evolution of plants and flowers.* Peter Lowe. ISBN 0–85654-024–2

Thomas, B. A. & Spicer, R. A. 1987. *The evolution and palaeobiology of land plants.* Croom Helm, London & Sydney. ISBN 0–931146-06–2, 0–931146-07–0

Tryon, R. M. & A. F. 1982. *Ferns and allied plants with special reference to tropical America.* Springer-Verlag, New York. ISBN 0–387–90672-x, 3–540-90672-x

White, M. E. 1988. *The greening of Gondwana.* Reed Books, New South Wales. ISBN 0–7301-0154–1

Rasbach, K., Rasbach, H. & Wilmanns, O. 1976 (2nd ed.). *Die Farnpflanzen Zentraleuropas.* Verlag, Stuttgart. ISBN 3–437–30223-x

PICTURE ACKNOWLEDGEMENTS

C. D. ADAMS p. 91 Bracken fronds
P. VON ADERKAS p. 90 Crozier of ostrich
fern : Croziers of ostrich fern on sale
G. ARGENT p. 84 *Dipteris conjugata*
p. 93 Tree-ferns
S. R. ASH p. 22 *Arnophyton kuesii*
E. A. BATES p. 104 Boston fern
G. BENL p. 56 *Bolbitis heudelotii*
Z. BRAMWELL p. 32 Mid-montane forest
D. M. BRITTON p. 71 *Pellaea glabella*
P. J. BROWNSEY p. 56 Shore spleenwort
(from *New Zealand Ferns and Allied
Plants*, David Bateman Ltd
J. E. BURROWS p. 29 *Mohria lepigera*
p. 32 *Xiphopteris villosissima*
p. 43 Stunted woodland, Zimbabwe
p. 53 Kariba water spangles
p. 71 *Cheilanthes involuta*
p. 83 *Cyathea dregei*
M. E. COLLINSON p. 24 *Azolla*
p. 25 *Acrostichum anglicum*
D. EDWARDS p. 18 *Cooksonia pertonii*
P. J. EDWARDS p. 10 *Psomiocarpa apiifolia*
T. C. T. EDWARDS pp 6–7 *Dicksonia
antarctica*
p. 14 *Diplazium proliferum*
D. R. FARRAR p. 11 Ribbon fern
p. 62 Rocky valley in Alabama
D. J. GALLOWAY pp. 78–79 Mount Osorno
J. GALTIER p. 19 *Psalixochlaena*
F. GREENAWAY p. 55 Dehisced 'pill' of the
pillwort
W. HAGEMANN p. 40 *Sphaerocionium*
p. 72 Nodding clubmoss, *Lycopodium
cernuum*
p. 76 *Isoetes velata*
p. 86 *Cryptogramma crispa* and *Athyrium
distentifolium*
E. HENNIPMAN p. 2 Stag's horn ferns
p. 9 *Dryopteris filix-mas* : *Cyrtomium*, a
holly fern : *Davallia*
p. 38 Ant-fern, *Lecanopteris carnosa*
p. 44 *Tapeinidium*
p. 47 Rhizome of ant-fern : Ant-fern
rhizome cut in half
J. M. HOBDAY p. 4 Epiphytic ferns
p. 8 Maidenhair fern
D. M. HOLLY p. 57 Mangrove fern
A. C. JERMY p. 3 Scaly male fern
p. 28 Bracket fern
p. 35 Clubmoss
p. 36 *Teratophyllum aculeatum*
p. 37 *Teratophyllum aculeatum*
p. 38 Ant-fern
p. 40 Clubmoss, *Selaginella involvens* :
Microgonium omphaloides : Unfurling
crozier of *Thelypteris*
p. 41 Mist forest
p. 42 Leaves of *Teratophyllum
clemensiae* : Hard fern, *Blechnum capense*
group
p. 43 Tree-ferns, Papua New Guinea
p. 44 Degraded land in Costa Rica
p. 45 Sword fern : Horsetail
p. 47 *Dipteris lobbiana*
pp. 48–49 Eventide on Loch Awe
p. 50 Spring quillwort

p. 51 Quillwort
p. 56 Water horsetail
p. 61 Primitive tree-fern
p. 66 Braid fern
p. 67 Roadside verge
p. 81 *Paramo*, Columbia
p. 82 *Isoetes andina*
p. 105 Clubmoss
D. L. JONES *Cover* and p. 64 Mother shield
fern
p. 104 Clubmoss
p. 105 Clubmoss
M. KATO p. 39 Mossy forest
p. 85 *Matonia foxworthyi*
C. B. KEATES p. 100 Cover of an album
J. KORNAS p. 50 Kariba water spangles
K. U. KRAMER p. 93 tree-fern vase
p. 96 Tree-fern stem tubs
T. LEMIEUX p. 8 *Cnemidaria horrida*
p. 30 Elephant's tongue
p. 71 *Notholaena sinuata*
p. 82 *Jamesonia canescens*
A. MEDWEEKA-KORNAS p. 74 *Actiniopteris
radiata* and *Selaginella imbricata* :
Selaginella imbricata
D. S. MITCHELL p. 51 Sepik River
T. NAKAIKE p. 65 *Polypodium lachnopus*
p. 82 *Papuapteris linearis*
NATURAL HISTORY MUSEUM p. 15
Quillwort
p. 21 *Lobatopteris miltonii* (Swiss) :
Lobatopteris miltonii (British) :
Asterotheca miltonii : Marattialean fern :
Palaeosmunda williamsii : *Cladophlebis
australis*
p. 23 *Protopteris punctata* : *Dicksonia
mariopteris* : *Phlebopteris smithii* :
Weichselia reticulata
p. 63 Killarney bristle fern
L. E. NEWTON p. 52 Mosquito fern
H. NISHIDA p. 30 Tree-fern, *Dicksonia
sellowiana*
p. 31 Filmy fern *Sphaerocionium* : Hand-
fern, *Cheiroglossa palmata*
pp. 58–59 *Blechnum cycadifolium*
p. 67 Tree-fern
B. ØLLGAARD *Inside back cover* and p. 31
Tree-fern
p. 34 Clubmoss
p. 80 *Huperzia trancilla* : *Huperzia
kuesteri*
p. 81 *Huperzia crassa*
S. S. OLSEN p. 103 Horsetail
C. N. PAGE p. 12 Horsetail
p. 60 Olympic Mountains
p. 63 Climbing fern, *Lygodium palmatum*
p. 85 *Gleichenia alpina*
pp. 98–99 Victorian fernery
A. M. PAUL p. 54 New Forest pool
G. S. PHILLIPS p. 55 Pillwort
C. J. PIGGOTT p. 15 Climbing fern
p. 28 Bird's nest ferns
p. 46 Button fern
p. 55 Water sprite
p. 70 Sword fern
C. M. POTTS *Inside front cover* and p. 106
Tree ferns

p. 106 *Blechnum marinum* : CV. 'foliosum
Moly's Green' : Shield fern
R. PRELLI p. 13 & 15 *Equisetum arvense*
p. 90 *Dryopteris filiix-mas*
p. 92 *Equisetum hyemale*
p. 94 *Asplenium trichomanes*
M. PROFUS p. 29 Miombo woodland
p. 72 *Actiniopteris pauciloba* : *Lycopodium
carolinianum*
p. 73 *Pellaea pectiniformis*
p. 75 *Cheilanthes inaequalis*
G. J. PROPER p. 11 Fern prothallus :
Sporeling fern
p. 87 Alpine habitat
p. 96 Maidenhair fern
H. & K. RASBACH p. 54 Clover-leaf fern
p. 61 Ferny *barranco*
p. 62 Maidenhair fern
p. 63 Verdon spleenwort
p. 64 Whisk fern
p. 75 *Asplenium ceterach*
p. 77 Clover-leaf fern
p. 86 *Cryptogramma crispa*
p. 87 *Botrychium lunaria*
p. 92 *Equisetum arvense*
p. 97 Stag's horn clubmoss
M. RICKARD p. 102 CVS 'ramo-cristata' :
'ramosum Felizor' and 'crispum'
p. 103 CV. 'divisilobum'
G. RODWAY p. 101 Wardian Case, People's
Palace Museum, Glasgow, reproduced
by kind permission of the Curator.
B. ROGERS p. 34 Elephant fern
M. C. ROOS p. 76 *Drynaria rigidula*
pp. 88–89 Flooded rice fields, Indonesia
E. SHEFFIELD p. 10 Necks of archegonia :
Antheridium
p. 90 Ostrich fern
p. 104 Bird's nest fern
J.-C. SMITH-DODSWORTH p. 46 *Tmesipteris
elongata* (from *New Zealand Ferns and
Allied Plants*, David Bateman Ltd.)
A. MCG. STERLING p. 85 *Woodsia alpina*
p. 86 *Polystichum lonchitis*
R. A. STOCKEY p. 25 *Onoclea sensibilis*
H. TAYLOR p. 52 Mosquito fern
p. 91 Bracken
B. A. THOMAS pp. 16–17 Giant clubmoss
base
p. 20 *Senftenbergia*
pp. 69–70 Las Canadas, Tenerife
R. N. TIMM p. 107 Royal fern
T. G. WALKER p. 33 Elephant fern,
Angiopteris
p. 93 Tree-fern stems
p. 95 Mosquito fern, *Azolla*
p. 100 Collage of ferns
J. W. WALLACE p. 12 Clubmoss,
Lycopodium
p. 14 Clubmoss bulbil
p. 64 Temperate rain forest
L. M. WARREN p. 70 *Cheilanthes vellea*
J. WATSON p. 20 *Psaronius*
Y. C. WEE p. 95 Scrambling fern
N. d'N. WINSER pp. 26–27 Gunung Mulu
National Park

FERN SOCIETIES

AUSTRALIA

The Fern Society of Victoria
PO Box 45
Heidelberg
Victoria 3081

Fern Society of Western Australia
c/o Mrs G. E. Bromley
73 Point Walter Road
Bicton
Western Australia 6157

Fern Society of South Australia Inc.
GPO Box 711
Adelaide
South Australia 5001

Tasmanian Fern Society
c/o Julie Haas
72 Bush Creek Road
Lenah Valley
Tasmania 7008

Sunshine Coast Fern Society
PO Box 47
Woombye
Queensland 4559

SGAP Fern Study Group
c/o Moreen Woolett
3 Currawang Place
Como West
New South Wales 2226

CHINA

The Fern Society of China
c/o Prof. K. H. Shing
Institute of Botany
Academia Sinica
Beijing 100044

INDIA

Indian Fern Society
c/o Prof. S. S. Bir
Department of Botany
Punjab University
Patiala 147 002

JAPAN

Japanese Pteridological Society
c/o Prof. K. Iwatsuki
Botanical Gardens
University of Tokyo
Hakusan 3–7–1
Bunkyo-Ku
Tokyo 112

Nippon Fernist Club
c/o Institute of Forest Botany
Faculty of Agriculture
University of Tokyo
Hongo
Bunkyo-ku
Tokyo 113

NETHERLANDS

Nederlandse Varenvereniging
c/o J. J. Comijs
Zaalboslaan 12
6881 RH Velp

NEW ZEALAND

Nelson Fern Society Inc. of New
Zealand
c/o Mrs J. Bonnington
9 Bay View Road
Atawhai
Nelson

Waikato Fern Club
c/o Mrs Eila McKenzie
164 Upper Dinsdale Road
Hamilton

PHILIPPINE ISLANDS

Fern Society of the Philippines
c/o National Museum
P. Burgos Street
Manilla

SWITZERLAND

Schweizerischen Vereinigung der
Farnfreunde
c/o Dr J. J. Schneller
Institüt für Systematische Botanik
Zollikerstrasse 107
CH-8008
Zürich

UNITED KINGDOM

The British Pteridological Society
c/o Miss A. M. Paul
Department of Botany
The Natural History Museum
Cromwell Road
London SW7 5BD

UNITED STATES OF AMERICA

American Fern Society
c/o Dr W. C. Taylor
Botany Dept.
Milwaukee Public Museum
800 W Wells Street
Milwaukee
Wisconsin 53233

Birmingham Fern Society
c/o Mrs R. E. Smith
4736 7th Avenue South
Birmingham
Alabama 35222

Corpus Christi Fern Society
c/o P. Coleman
438 Claremont Street
Corpus Christi
Texas 78412

Delaware Valley Fern Society
c/o Mrs M. B. Peterson
22 West Southampton Avenue
Philadelphia
Pennsylvania 19118

Fern Study Group of the Northwest
Horticultural Society
c/o Mr N. Hall
1230 North East 88th Street
Seattle
Washington 98115

International Tropical Fern Society
c/o 14895 Gardenhill Drive
La Mirada
California 90638

Los Angeles International Fern Society
PO Box 90943
Pasadena
California 91109–0943

Louisiana Fern Society
c/o F. H. Yeargers
901 Robert E. Lee Boulevard
New Orleans
Louisiana 70124

Memphis Fern Society
c/o Ms B. Feuerstein
2357 Thornwood Lane
Memphis
Tennessee 38138

Southwestern Fern Society
c/o Mrs M. Duncan
3014 San Paula
Dallas
Texas 75228

West Florida Fern Society
c/o Dr M. Cousens
Department of Biology
University of West Florida
Pensacola
Florida 32504